Married

Married

A Fine Predicament

Anne Roiphe

BASIC
BOOKS

A MEMBER OF THE PERSEUS BOOKS GROUP

Designed by Lovedog Studio

The Library of Congress has cataloged the hardcover edition as follows:

Roiphe, Anne Richardson, 1935-

Married : a fine predicament / [Anne Roiphe]

p. cm.

ISBN 0-465-07066-3 (alk. paper)

1. Marriage. I. Title.

HQ734 .R7135 2002

306.81—dc21

2002003506

ISBN 0-465-07067-1 (pbk.)

03 04 / 10 9 8 7 6 5 4 3 2 1

To Rachel Herz-Roiphe

The world was all before them, where to choose
Their place of rest, and Providence their guide:
They hand in hand with wand'ring steps and slow,
Through Eden took their solitary way.

PARADISE LOST, John Milton 1674

Acknowledgments

I want to thank Liz Maguire for working with me in wise friendship and Lisa Bankoff for her clear counsel and Alan and Ellen Isler for bringing me to John Milton. I thank Dr. Fred Pine for conversations that mattered and Arlene S. Skolnick whose books informed this work. I thank most especially Dr. Herman Roiphe whose voice is in all I do.

Chapter 1

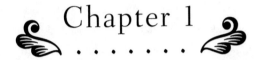

The Worry

As the mother of daughters some of them still unmarried I noticed that I was reading the wedding announcements with an indecent amount of attention. I read descriptions of weddings of people I didn't know and would never know as if hidden in the lines were a secret code that if I could decipher would bring my children to their own marriages. Beneath my fascination I found envy lurking. I thought of myself as a lighthouse standing on the shore flashing my beam across a stretch of dark ocean, attempting to guide their ships into a safe harbor. This was particularly absurd because I know as well as the next person that marriage is just the beginning of the story; afterwards comes the plot, the work, the place where shipwrecks occur routinely. I know better than to think that marriage is the only or right path to happiness and yet I felt anxiety: what would become of them? My anxiety irritated my daughters of course. It irritated me.

In a sore place a book begins.

The idea of a sanctioned union between the sexes begins in Genesis when God sees Adam and sees that he is lonely. "'It is not good,' saith He, 'that man should be alone. I will make him a helpmeet for him.'" Never mind the patriarchy in that description, never mind that Darwin tells the story with greater balance between the sexes and more credibility, the basic idea is right. It is not good to go through life alone. In my childhood we played card games in which the object was not to be stuck with the Old Maid card. Her picture was appalling, hair askew, a pinched face, tight mouth, and long baggy dress. This is now a politically incorrect image precisely because it was so intimidating. It evoked pity and scorn and fear in equal proportions and was directed at the female. This was absurd. Of course your life is not miserable if you do not marry or do not stay married. Of course you need not look like a frump or live without love because you didn't get to that altar. In more coercive times the image of the old maid was a threat meant to keep every little girl in line. Today she isn't an old maid anymore but a career girl in her late thirties nervously searching for a mate in order to have children before her biological clock gives way to menopause. She is no longer the butt of the joke but has been transformed into one of the heroines of "Sex in the City," sharing the common fear of so many that they will miss out or be left out. There is something in the sad singleness of Adam before there was Eve, reflected in all the men and women who do not, as did all the animals of God's kingdom, go two by two into the ark. There is something fearful in human life without coupling. There is also something fearful in coupling. No doubt you take your life in your hands when you marry: also if you don't.

Just imagine—we remove marriage from the landscape. Boys and girls grow up expecting to cohabit or not, to have children or not, to take care of themselves in times of sickness, to save for their own old age and live out their lives free of divorce, free of obligations. Imagine a world in which children are raised in communal houses by senior citizens. Right now twelve-year-olds live like this, roaming the playground in packs, whispering secrets to a best friend, finding out what they like and what they don't, making plans for futures that will surely be different from the present. Add sexual experience to this vision and you see a world of adults with no reason not to change everything in their lives on a whim, with expectations of other choices ever blooming, ever tempting. In this world no one person works to put another through school. In this world banks grant mortgages based on one tax return only. No one feels fear of being left out (always a bridesmaid never a bride), and gays and lesbians are able to link or unlink with one another in the same manner as everyone else. In this world the wedding industry loses and divorce lawyers drop below the poverty line and couples therapists starve, the Elvis Chapel in Las Vegas shuts its doors, but the rest of us go about our days rich in friends and lovers, our lives sanctified by God and State not at any particular moment but always. Is this utopia or is it hell?

There is abroad in the land an acute anxiety about marriage. We all know that only 25 percent of Americans are living in

traditional families. Only 51 percent of all children live in
two-parent homes. The proportion of all households headed
by married couples fell from 77 percent in 1950 to 55 percent
in 1993. Today 36 percent of children are living apart from
their biological fathers compared with only 17 percent in
1960. The divorce rate in 1998 was twice as high as it was in
1968. We know that divorce is as common as the cold. We
know that even Baptist ministers in the Deep South are concerned that so many of their weddings end in disaster. The
age of marriage is climbing so high that we can see the day
when only the long in tooth and short on the future make it to
the altar. We know that vast numbers of women and a few
good men are raising children without spouses and that in
most parts of the country both men and women have sex
whenever they wish without benefit of state or religious sanc-
tion. The bookstores are filled with medicines for troubled
marriages: a sure sign of epidemic misery among us. Hucksters
and shamans make fortunes off of any promise to heal a troubled marriage. We have lost confidence that marriage will make
us happy, that marriage is a blessing. Many young men and
women are afraid of the so-called "commitment." They stall.
They wait. They have seen unhappy parents split and wander.
Like a child afraid to dive into the pool they shiver at the edge
uncertain. So the question arises: do we still need marriage
and if we do what do we need it for? Is there anything we can
do about the sorry state of our domestic lives? Are we on the
way to phasing out marriage as a social, cultural, religious
necessity? Are we in a transitional period and if so what
comes next?

Strangely enough after some years of marriages held barefoot on the beach we are now seeing the return of the very fancy traditional wedding, the bride and groom figures resting on top of a big white cake, the most expensive flowers, the very dazzling dress. These formal ceremonies serve like sandbags at the levee. They make a brave statement. "We will not be swept away in the heavy floodwaters of contemporary chaos and confusion. We will close our eyes and pretend it is 1950 and perhaps it will be." The popular fancy wedding can be understood as an anxious symptom of the current marital malaise. Perhaps a bachelor party, add a bachelorette party, a white dress, a florist's handiwork, can make our vows indelible, turn the evil eye away from our bans.

Another sign of our anxiety is the fierce resistance of the religious right to gay and lesbian marriage. This reveals not so much meanness as sheer fright. If marriage were a strong institution it would not be placed in peril by loving homosexual couples joining in. The anger and the anxiety caused in parts of this country by the very idea of a gay marital vow tells us just how fragile our social system seems, how it totters and shakes before the winds of change. Some are worried the respect for marriage may be slipping down a new cultural drain. That's why they call so loudly for women's obedience, for abstinence before the wedding night, for "family values." But the old world where marriage kept a woman in her place and sex was a genie kept inside of the bottle (or so we pretended) is disappearing, has in most parts of the country already disappeared. The conservative hysteria on the subject is a measure of how severely our marriages are truly under siege. No wonder the conservative right is fighting back. No wonder there are significant backlashes—no wonder reactionary talk-show hosts speak of feminazis and speak of gays as if they were communist saboteurs attempting the overthrow of all we hold dear.

There are however family values that are not those "family values." There are other family values that are humane, flexible, and yet strong. These values too have deep roots although those roots are not necessarily planted in the authority of a deity. They do not require a return to an America of another era. I believe my daughters, raised by a feminist and a psychoanalyst, could one day arrive at marriages that maintain the best of the past and shed the worst. Do they believe that, can they find a mate? That is the question.

The Way It Was

When I was twenty-one and just graduated from college I was in love with a daring, dashing young man who wanted to be a writer. He spoke with an English accent of his own invention having been raised in a one-bedroom apartment in an outer borough of Manhattan by a divorced mother and divorced grandmother whose family or some other branch of the family had once had money in the state of South Carolina. He wanted to be famous the way some boys want to be baseball players. That is, very seriously. He was nervous like an Arabian horse. He was beautiful like one too. He drank not simply too much but constantly. I thought all artists did. He knew volumes of poetry by heart. He was a philosophy student. He allowed me to buy him drinks and sometimes to drive him home across the bridge to Queens after the bars had closed. He won a fellowship to Germany and asked me to go with him. Perhaps he didn't so much ask as allowed it. I stole a ring from my mother's jewelry box the proceeds from the sale of which allowed him to go to Europe with me three months before his fellowship began.

In Paris that summer we moved into a small apartment on Boulevard Montparnasse. He was writing a long story about a graduate student who shot his philosophy professor for destroying his faith in God. I was sitting in cafes watching the passing scene. My mother thought I was traveling with friends, who mailed her postcards every now and then that I had prewritten. As August approached I knew I wanted to go to Munich with my roommate, my partner. He was a writer. I was his muse. The year was 1957. I wrote my mother and told her the truth about my whereabouts and asked her to send me my winter coat, also some money. She wrote back and said if I was going to Munich I should get married. My lover disappeared for a two-day binge when presented with that idea but then he agreed.

We got a license and had a civil ceremony at the town hall of the arrondissement in which we were living. There were many couples waiting to be married in the large room before the mayor's bench. Many of the brides were in white and about to go off to their church weddings. I had on my best dress which was somewhat wrinkled because I didn't have an iron, nor did I know how to use one. When it was our turn we

stood before the mayor and he said the necessary civil words
and then he leaned over his bench and loudly called out in
English to us, "You know I have never in all the twenty years
that I have been mayor of this arrondissement, had any marriage of mine end in divorce." He was congratulating himself
and us, that was clear from his tone of voice. I remember,
although that was forty-four years ago, the sharp pang of guilt
that ran through me at his words. I was in love, could have
done only what I did, and still I knew standing there that I
might well produce his first marital failure. All day long I felt
ashamed that I might ruin this mayor's perfect record. When
six years later I held my divorce papers in my hand in a court-
house in Juarez, Mexico, and the clerk who stamped them
wished me, "Felice dia," I wondered if the mayor of my
arrondissement would find out. I hoped not.

   In 1957 I couldn't live in sin and grow up at my own pace.
In 1957 I didn't dare. Ten years later I wouldn't have been so
sure that my only option was to marry a writer when I wanted
to be one myself. I have no nostalgia for the past or for those
who would keep others in ancient prisons simply because the
present is so chaotic, confusing, and not yet satisfactory.

Anxious but Undeterred

This anxiety about marriage has not yet killed the idea of marriage. The achievement of a happy marriage, of a love-filled
home, is still a core value, a deeply desired and sought-after
ideal. This wish exists equally in secular urban centers among

those bearing Ph.D.'s and LL.D.'s and M.D.'s as well as in the distant corners of Pat Robertson country and under the big skies of the far west and southwest. Marriage remains a crucial life plan for most of us and achieving legal state-sanctioned marriage is still a sign of belonging to one's community, and taking one's adult place in the world no matter how unsteady that world or that place may seem. If the folks who did the census that discovered that only 25 percent of Americans are living in nuclear units could have measured the number of those who would like to, women and men who want families or want a partner to parent with them but haven't figured it out yet, the 25 percent would take one giant leap upward. This is not a provable statement but does anyone doubt it? We still have images of happy homes dancing in our heads, no matter how crackling the cyberspace around us becomes. We want our children to have a Ma and a Pa just like Mary, Laura and Carrie, in "Little House on the Prairie." This is our conflict. Reality clashes with wish, myth with fact. It makes us nervous and it should.

It is not just for future children that we marry. It is for ourselves.

Plato told the tale that once upon a time the human being was both male and female, a one-in-all creature, and then we were split apart and both halves spend their lives looking for the other half to make themselves complete. This it turns out is rotten science but adequate metaphor. There is something in us that longs for union, if not merger with the other sex, that feels complete in this mating satisfied in both its physical and emotional impact. However this perfect union, this recreation of ourselves as one double sexed being, is no easy matter. It requires fusing both our erotic love and our minds into another person's body. It means placing erotic love and companionship in the same place. Even Dr. Freud may have found this slightly beyond his grasp. His wife, who became the dutiful Viennese mother and housekeeper, appears not to have been the ideal intellectual companion he also needed. For that it seems he preferred his unmarried sister-in-law Minna Bernays and then later his daughter Anna. Martha Freud was left outside at least when it came to discussing his ever flowing ideas, his professional colleagues, his true interests in archeology, art history, and science. If this is truly so, poor Martha, poor Sigmund. They neither of them succeeded in finding the wholeness Plato glimpsed. This is not because Freud lived much of his life in a pre-Freudian era. It is because Plato's ideal is unrealistic, especially so in societies in which women are so often relegated to the tasks of the home and men are sent out into the world growing apart from their wives. That Freud seems to have found a way to live happily with three women attending him, two not married to anyone else, is perhaps proof of his genius.

This view of completeness served by marriage is also in the Talmud. We find this in the commentary. "Why did the Torah state, 'if any man take a wife' (Deuteronomy 22:13) and not 'if a woman be taken to a man'?" Because, says R. Simeon, "it is the way of man to go in search of a woman, but it is not the way of a woman to go in search of a man. This may be compared to a man who lost an article: who goes in search of whom? The loser goes in search of the lost article. (Thus man having lost his rib, he seeks to recover it.)" Never mind that this reflects the sexist courtship practices of several thousands of years right up to the present. It also tells us that the rib story is a form of the Plato fable. We feel incomplete one without the other. In some ways man and woman, husband and wife, are one being.

Of course this oneness is tricky. Taken too literally the Platonic ideal can ruin a marriage. Too much oneness and someone may disappear into the other, which is not good for the survival of the marriage. Marriage cannot make a person with a seriously sick soul well. It cannot fill in all the holes we have or serve to keep us alive like a mind meld on "Star Trek." The two-into-one process in the sense that Plato meant it needs a lot of balance and explanation and caution in the modern world. As a metaphor it works well enough to describe the sexual act but fails to capture the nature of companionship which by definition requires a twoness as well as a oneness.

Ah, a paradox, a headache: no wonder most of us are confused—what is it we agreed to at the altar? Did we know what we were doing?

Given that most women these days do not think of themselves as helpmeets and certainly do not feel their purpose in life is to behave like another person's rib, supporting their mate's breathing apparatus, it is amazing that weddings still take place and any new families start up like shoots of evergreens in the soil of a burnt-out forest, but they do, they do.

It could be some of us marry because if you live in a railroad station sooner or later you board a train and the idea of marriage while undermined remains the dominant image, the shopworn instructions given to all on how to live. But it might also be that we marry because despite so many pieces of evidence to the contrary we still hope beyond hope that our lives can hold a soulmate, a friend who is both erotic partner and companion, who will stand with us as bulwark against the tides of disaster, the erosion of time. The persistence of that hope in the face of modern evidence is remarkable and perhaps a sign that despite the great evils done by man to woman, woman to man, we do have souls that yearn for better things. That hope dies hard. Some of us, including me, have married several times because of it.

Diehards

On the eve of my thirty-fourth anniversary my husband and I go out to dinner at our favorite restaurant. I hold his hand under the table. Our conversation is slow and usual. We worry the same things over again. We make plans for a trip we are taking. We discuss the other people in the restaurant. An idea floats through my mind. What if I hadn't married him? What if I had gone down to Appalachia and become a public health nurse as I had imagined I might as I lived through a 1967 version of "Sex in the City," putting my baby to sleep on the coats in strangers' bedrooms night after night? What if I had simply lived from affair to affair with married men and amused myself on lonely nights with English poetry? I might be better read but would I be happier? If you take one road you can never know what lay waiting down the other, a fatal car accident on a highway in South Carolina or something that might have brought me to a life as an expatriate poet in a town on the Sicilian coast? Who knows?

On our anniversary I looked across the table over my champagne glass at my husband and he smiled at me. I saw the same shy, sweet smile I had noticed across a room at a party in the long distant past when I was still close to my childhood and planning my memoirs because I didn't know that my life was just beginning as people at the beginning don't and he was a divorced doctor with two young children about whom he talked with animal ferocity and a lump of hard pain in his throat.

My anniversary is a day of true thanksgiving, of gratitude for the luck that came, for the path I took. I say to him, "Promise me our daughters will find mates." He laughs. "They will be all right," he says as he always says. "Alone?" I say. "Yes," he says. "Alone or not they will be all right. Times are changing. They are independent, educated, strong women. They will make a good life. Trust them." "I don't," I say. "I know," he says. I hate the way he takes the long view when I can hardly see beyond my nose. I love his long view. It comforts me through the night.

Tears of Happiness?

A wedding is the one place where joy is guaranteed and many people can't help crying. This tincture of sadness in the midst of a happy occasion is an interesting matter. Of all the people who might be wiping tears from their eyes, no two are proba-

bly shedding them for exactly the same reasons. A different
phrase of the liturgy, when the bride enters or the groom fum-
bles to find the ring, or the flower girl stumbles on her way
down the central aisle, can begin a sniffling in the audience, a
clogging of the nose of the mother of the bride, a mist on the
eyeglasses of the father of the groom and a choking sobbing
sound coming from a new acquaintance of the family who was
just invited at the last moment.

These mysterious but common tears seem to flow from the
intensity of emotion but more likely they spring from some
fountain of self-pity. "I once had a moment as pure as this and
look where I have come." These are tears for lost youth, lost
love, lost grace, for the time in one's life when everything lay
before one and the real endurance tests were waiting silently
in the wings. These tears may also rise because we know by
bitter experience that despite the beauty of the ceremony, the
love of the family surrounding the bride and groom, there is no
way to protect the young couple from the struggles ahead. Will
they lose a child to illness? Will they be unable to conceive
and turn on each other in their disappointment? Will he lose
his job? Will she lose hers? Will he or she fall in love with
someone else? Will he or she prove unworthy of the trust now
placed in their person? The list of real world traps, obstacles,
emotional minefields is endless and particular to each of us.
Everybody over the age of ten knows that like the evil unin-
vited fairy at Sleeping Beauty's party Divorce lies somewhere
in the wings waiting, laughing at us. That's enough to bring a
tear to a person's eye.

Some people cry because the ideal, "till death do us part," seems so painfully beautiful. The beauty is in the long time it takes to get to the parting. The pain is obvious. Some people think of their own deaths, others think of their own partings. Some people are jealous of the young lovers and this jealousy forms itself into tears of self-pity. Some people never cry at weddings because they never allow such feelings to approach consciousness. These are not the lucky ones. These are the ones who have looked at Medusa's head and turned into stone.

I will cry at my daughters' weddings. The task before me is not to cry or whine or protest to an uncaring universe if there are no weddings.

Practical Matters, or Love of Money

Sentiment aside marriage is as the anthropologists have said a kinship system. Love is a word we use to cover a mess of calculations that were more baldly apparent in Jane Austen's day but are with us still. Which is not to say that romantic love doesn't play its part only that it is prodded, encouraged, inflamed by certain other considerations that one might call social opportunity. Love can be the attractive container for advancement, financial or social, sort of like putting medicine in an elaborately sculpted perfume bottle. Marriage is still the easiest way to satisfy some ambitions. The calculated right choice can pole vault a person to the top rung of society's ladder or right into the pot of gold at the end of the rainbow. The opposite is also true. The society pages of our local newspaper tell of daughters of bankers and investment counselors marrying the gardener or the stable groom, sons marrying nannies or shopgirls (referred to in the announcements as landscape artists and managers of a horse stable, childcare workers, etc.). If there is enough money the partner with the lower status has simply come up in the world, but if there is not, the bride will do her own dishes and her children will attend local schools and life will be hard for the couple as it is always hard for those without trust funds, education, or daredevil ingenuity.

Once upon a time when I was very young I thought that all talk of money and security was crude and rude. I thought the only thing that mattered was love itself. That is what we tell each other in America. It is certainly what we tell the children. The movies tell us that this is so. The television dramas remind us with weekly regularity that to be rich in Dallas or L.A. is like putting your head in a shark's mouth. Every American third grader knows that you are not supposed to say nasty things to the fat boy in front of the teacher or admit you don't want to give a portion of your allowance to the poor. With this level of conviction they also know that you are supposed to believe that character is a far more important attribute than money. On the other hand no one believes that those supermodels would marry Donald Trump if he was a shoe salesman at a store in the mall or that all those trophy wives one sees on the streets of Palm Beach would have loved their spouses if all their wealth had been given away to the local hospital. I wonder if I would have fallen in love with my own spouse if he had asked me to take my child and join him in a trailer park. Wasn't it his education and his success in America that was a part of what I admired about him? I loved him because he was a healer of hurt souls but would I have loved him if he did his healing as part of a voodoo ritual for which he was paid in rabbit skins?

It is ironic that we in this most materialistic country in the world, grand producer of the consumer culture, capitalists all, believe with childish enthusiasm in the absolute supremacy and infinite goodness of romantic love or so we say. Yet if you marry for love alone you may be left with blisters on your soul as well as on your hands. Without a modicum of financial security the thing called love may get crushed like a butterfly in the claws of the cat. Every grown-up knows that. Every grown-up also knows that with financial security the thing called love may still get crushed like a butterfly in the claws of the cat.

My mother used to say, "It's just as easy to love a rich man as a poor one." For some people it's easier than for others. My mother, a rich woman herself in fact, married a poor man and paid a high price for his cold opportunism. When I was very young I thought money was evil and poverty was a kind of virtue especially if you painted pictures or sung arias in your unheated garret. I saw first hand throughout my childhood the uselessness of pretty things when you lacked affection. All the fine china in the world cannot supply a pleasant meal. Our dinners in my childhood home were eaten on an art deco blonde wooden table selected to go with a Chinese screen chosen by the interior decorator for our wall. The maid passed the roast beef on a silver platter. But the adults called each other nasty names. The children stared at their plates and wished they were elsewhere. My mother often said that she would give up all her money to live in harmony with a decent man in a shack by the railroad tracks. She didn't do that. Her path never crossed that of the man with the shack. He was not to be found in the aisles of Saks Fifth Avenue, more's the pity.

She wanted me to marry a man with money for comfort and protection from the winds of misfortune. She believed both in the value of hard cash and the romantic ideal. She split the two beliefs apart and maintained them both with equal ardor. In this she was a typical American, inconsistent, illogical, but exactly like everyone else.

Personally, as a teenager, I thought that the wealth of the country ought to be redistributed so that it was spread out in an equal fashion across the land. I purchased copies of the *Daily Worker* which I hid under my pillow where the maid would find them and throw them out. I also hoped that the world might change so love too could come to those who were without. That was my secret revolutionary goal.

In my second marriage we have often had trouble over money. My mate grew up during the terrible depression of the 1930s and he is frugal and cautious. I am ever hopeful that more money will come from somewhere. Neither of us is very good at real financial investments or plans. We balance each other out. His unrealistic caution tempers my absurd optimism. My optimism tempers his caution. And sometimes we make bad mistakes together for which we try not to blame each other. But at times when tuition bills have been high and extra strains are placed on our budget there is a tension between us that might erupt into something really bad if we aren't very careful.

I lie sometimes and reduce the price of something I've bought. While this is only a little white lie it is not good, but worse would be his grief and concern and anger over what may or may not be my extravagance. He is not happy if I buy him a present of any value at all. I have learned not to make him unhappy with my gifts. I would have taken more trips, ridden in more taxicabs, indulged in more luxuries but for the sorrow and worry this would cause him. He is silent and withdraws from me when he is worrying about money. This makes me angry. It's a kind of fight. Our worst financial mistakes came about because we couldn't realistically see how worried we should or should not be in a given situation. But I imagine many people fight about money and worry when they should-n't and don't worry when they should because money and security are such relative matters and how we feel about them is based on our earliest experiences. We all transfer our most basic fears onto money which is why we find the richest peo-ple holding on to pennies as if their life depended on their piggy banks. Almost no one is entirely rational when it comes to money which is odd considering that there is nothing magi-cal about funds in and funds out.

"Marry for money and you earn it," Oscar Wilde says. But marrying without thinking about money can leave you thinking about money all the time.

In every marriage there are regrets that are about money. Once I sold my grandmother's emerald pin because we needed money for special schooling for one of our children that at the time we thought essential. Later I realized the sale hadn't been necessary. We could have managed without selling the pin which could never be retrieved. I think the loss of this pin was his fault; his excessive worry drove me to it. On the other hand perhaps we really had no choice. I remember the back-room office of the jewelry store where I handed the pin over and received a check. I was sitting in a big red leather chair. There was a wedding photograph on the man's desk. His daughter, he said. It was long ago and doesn't really matter but a mark is left on our marriage, a little shadow lingers there.

We often fall in love with someone who will give us the life we want to lead. This may mean something solid like a lot of money but it may also mean something innocent and personal like a life spent in learning at a university or a life in the military or a life on a farm or a life of travel. Our loves tend to follow our wishes for ourselves. Why not? Whom we marry affects our status in the community. It affects our personal wealth or prospects for security. All our songs are about romantic love, finding it or losing it, but we fool ourselves if we confuse Nashville's Ole Opry with the real business of living. Even in the twenty-first century marriage places you, marks you, labels you, folds you more firmly than ever before into your social class and economic place, pushes you into a religious group or subgroup. In this it is different from merely living with a partner. Whom you marry is a large part of who you are in our society. While whom you share a bathroom with is merely your own concern or the concern of those who love you, and leaves little trace on your social identity.

This is less true when the age of marriage is postponed until both partners have achieved their own places in the world but even then there are social risks and rewards in choosing a mate. Like the honeycombs of bees, society has a little hole for each of us. There is no escaping that. Which is not to imply that every marriage is sweet.

The Poor Have No Monopoly on Misery

There are sociologists who write on family life who believe that economics has a great deal to do with how well we can love our mates and how stable our marriages are. They point to the fact that among lower-wage-earning families marriages have an even harder time than in the general public. Close to thirty years ago Daniel Patrick Moynihan observed that material poverty and job loss put an unbearable strain on marriages. Men who do not have jobs tend to drift away from their wives, girlfriends and children. Without being able to provide for their families they become prey to alcohol or drugs, they end up in prison or simply deserting the home. Without the pride of a wage earner they may abuse their wives in order to regain some sense of manhood, express power over someone when they are so powerless. These sociologists see in our vast inequality of wealth a set-up for marriage disaster among certain parts of our population. They say that our corporate culture makes no room for family life, for the sickness of a spouse, for the time a parent needs to be with a new baby, for the need of men and women to find time to be together. They find lack of adequate funds to be a pressure on parents that may cause them to take second jobs that take them out of the home for too many hours of the week.

All this may be so. But hard times, struggle to make it, to feed the children, to keep a roof over your head, to meet the mortgage, to save a little, have been part of the human experience in every country, in every age, in every era. When we were hunters and gatherers herds were hunted to extinction. When we planted crops locusts came. When we had farms they were inundated by floodwaters. When we needed rain it didn't come. It is not just capitalism that makes earning a living wage, providing for a family hard. And marriages in all geographies and eras have always either bent as the willow tree with the wind or broken apart as the wooden hull of a ship caught in a terrible storm at sea.

But in addition the very wealthy and the highly educated have a high divorce rate, and sometimes a sense of privilege and entitlement serves to encourage people to divorce at the first sign of difficulty, to follow through on carefully worded prenups and to break up homes as if they were tea cups on the table. Men who are perfectly competent wage earners fall into depressions or substance abuse or just wandering habits. Women who can shop at the mall for designer shoes grow dissatisfied with their lot in life, yearn for greater intimacy with their mates, cry in bed at night because they are not touched in the right way. Economic inequality is not a good thing but it is not to blame for most of our marital troubles.

It would be a better world if everyone had a decent job and all wage earners could depend on their wages and factories would never close and corporations would all have on-site day care and the working commute would be shorter and good housing available to all. But I suspect that marriages would still shake and quiver just as they always have. We are a species not so easily made happy.

The conservatives think our failure to keep people in marriages, to get them married in the first place, is a sign of our moral corruption. The liberals think it is a sign of our brutal and uncaring economic system. I am not convinced that we were morally finer when women married still in their teens and suffered in bad marriages for all their lives. I am not sure that children were raised better when prejudice against homosexuals was so strong that people hid in closets. I am not sure that children were raised better when fathers worked long hours out of the home and were known to their children only as disciplinarians or as shadow figures. Homes with depressed or isolated women were not better homes than those created by single parents. And the option not to marry at all is an advance, not a setback, for the dignity of the human soul. The appearance of normality always covered a mess of discomfort. No news there.

Marriage as an institution is neither moral nor immoral: no more than an umbrella or a pagoda or a dollar bill.

What may be moral or immoral is what occurs within marriage between the partners. And here matters become too complex for religion or economics or politics to solve, not that they haven't tried.

Who Is That Person in My Bed?

We are often surprised by our own choices. We almost never get exactly what we thought we were getting. Not just in our life plans, which can be drastically affected by real events of all kinds, from illness to job promotion to sudden tragedy, but also in our mates. Their characters, their souls, will most certainly not be exactly what we were expecting. Because the human mind is too full of crevices, secrets, pressures, a landscape of minefields and wants and unspoken unknowable needs that will emerge as the days and years pass. We are bound to be surprised by our mates, both happily and unhappily.

Thirty-four years ago I was sitting on a blanket at the edge of an August ocean watching my very young daughter from a marriage now two years gone running back and forth in the white foam like a sandpiper, all bone and sinew. She rushed forward and then quickly retreated with the incoming tide, hair wild in the wind, her small screams of joy and terror or terror and joy lost in the pounding sound of the waves. I let the sun warm my shoulder blades and with my hands I covered my feet with soft damp sand. I was in love. I was planning to get married again. This man was not like the first man. This man was older, far wiser, sweeter, calmer, a psychoanalyst unruffled by the ruder parts of my being and willing to care for me and my child. Think of it, I could have a psychoanalyst for my very own, one who would never say, "Our time is up." My love for him was like a secret code I alone could decipher. It was now a burden to wait for him in the evenings. I had to stop myself from calling him frequently during the day. When something

happened to me I told it to him immediately if only in my
head. When he smiled I felt triumphant. When he turned distant and retreated into his own thoughts I felt the proverbial
footsteps on my grave. Had I been abandoned? I counted the
minutes till he returned to me. I had been afraid he didn't love
me back, admire me, lust for me as I for him. But he did.

Even in the midst of this tender new love I wondered there
on the beach, what will be wrong in this union? How long will
it take me to find out why he needs me and I need him and
what is not so honest, not so beautiful in our love? Because I
knew by then, I was thirty years old, that the demons in my
soul could fool my judgment, would surely produce surprises
of an unpleasant sort. I knew by then that no man was without
his flaws and my own defects were if not totally clear at least
becoming apparent to me. What would time reveal when we
were married that I couldn't imagine now no matter how hard
I tried, here at the cusp of this wedding? I remember the not
quite innocence of that moment. I remember his coming up
behind me and the voices of his two children as they spread
their towels around me. I knew I would marry him, risking my
future and my child's future because I hoped too much, loved
too much to do otherwise and could not imagine life without
marriage despite personal experience that might have discour-
aged me. Also I wanted more children. I wanted a family the
way a person lost in the desert wants a drink of water.

But I knew I didn't know him, really know him. Not
because love is blind but because only in the unfolding of the
days, the running into bad spots, the tests that would come
our way, the shifts in power that occur in relationships, would

he gradually become known to me and I to him. This early knowing, this early loving, was just the prologue. I was still pretending to be able to cook a decent meal and he hadn't told me yet what scared him most of all. I hadn't yet seen him lose his temper. He still thought it charming that I never entered checks in the checkbook. I thought he would right my listing child and he hoped his not-so-friendly oldest daughter would embrace me.

The year was 1967. I was swimming against the incoming current which was bringing us a dream of free-wheeling sexual play and open marriages and flower children and "Lucy in the Sky with Diamonds." This was the dark ages for the "family values" holdouts. The culture was truly coming unhinged, reeling from idea to idea. Everywhere Authority (political, military, university, religious) had egg on its face, and everywhere people were calling naughty things nice and nice things naughty. In the media the family appeared to be under siege.

Women were out there spitting. The anger expressed everywhere cleared the sinus's ah! Marriage wasn't a sanctuary anymore. It was seen as a dangerous place where a woman could lose her identity and her personal gifts. I didn't care, perhaps too much a child of the fifties, perhaps not tough enough to brave the world alone.

We were married at a friend's apartment. During the ceremony the Rabbi expressed his dislike of my just published first novel. My daughter, dressed in blue velvet with a delicate lace collar, would not sit still or stop talking or tugging at my dress. We took the three not quite comfortable children on our honeymoon with us. We didn't want anyone to feel left out of our new union. By the time we returned home some of my family members who had read my first novel were no longer speaking to me. Soon his ex-wife was screaming at him over the telephone every other day. Although this was not an auspicious beginning we were determined to make good things grow around us, never mind the toxic soil in which our marriage was planted, in which most second chances begin.

Did we really know each other when we began? We each took a leap across a chasm. We trusted what we could not verify. There were surprises, good and bad.

Is It Old-Fashioned If Love Lasts?

At this point I've been married for thirty-four years to the same man. We put together a family. His two daughters by his first marriage and my one daughter. Then we had two more girls. I thought it would be far easier than it was. I thought that love would suffice to smooth the way. I thought I was up to anything life could toss at me. I wasn't. We have had many crises and troubles along the way and our love for one another did little to prevent them. What it did do was to hold us together, make a safe place in each other's arms where we could float and drift and find our way.

One day I was walking on Riverside Drive along the park and on the cobblestones I saw a pigeon lying dead, its grey feathers flattened and dulled blowing in the slight breeze. Around the pigeon I saw a second pigeon moving in frantic circles; every few steps it would stop and peck at the dead pigeon as if it were trying to raise the dead. As I watched the circles got faster and faster and the distress of the surviving pigeon was obvious. It was a horrible sight. There is no way to offer comfort to a pigeon who has lost its mate. The trees by the park are old and very tall and across the stone wall I could see the river moving toward the harbor and the high-rise apartment buildings of New Jersey. On the river a long garbage barge was moving slowly toward the Jersey side. Nothing in the near universe as far as the eye could see cared about the death of this pigeon except the other pigeon, its mate. If this much feeling is a mere pigeon's portion think what we human beings have to gain and lose in marriage.

Chapter 2

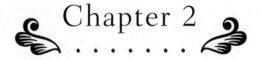

Is It Cool If It Falls Apart?

For some being married is like being born again as a tree
standing next to another tree, branches intertwined, sun and
rain and wind striking both alike, seasons changing, expanding
outward and upward, interlocking roots reaching deep into the
earth. For others being married is like being handcuffed to
another, while bumping, dragging along on a forced march in
the wrong direction. Look at the world around us, everywhere
we see tribe set against tribe, massacres, wars, genocides,
mass burials in ditches by the side of roads. There are now and
have been for all of recorded history coups and revolutions and
fights physical and otherwise over land and money. Since man
dropped from the trees the most minor of religious differences
have led to bloodshed or banishment. The tale of Cain and
Abel is not outdated. We know how very hard if not impossible
it is for human beings to get along with each other with

mutual affection and constant empathy. And it's not just in groups that we behave like one of Lucifer's band of banished angels. We are creatures who want our own needs satisfied, and our impulses for domination, power, rile us, drive us, hide there right behind our most treasured institutions. It is not only the rallying cries of church, state or army that can set us off like banshees in the dark of jungle night. Each of us wants, personally, the entire cake and finds it hard to settle for a mere slice. Impulses to destroy those who are in our way are planted deep down in the foundations of our souls. Thomas Hobbes called it right in his book *Leviathan* written in 1651. He said we need the state to control our savage nature, our desire to steal, to murder, to destroy. Without a covenant with the state in which we give up some of our freedoms we would devour each other in endless acts of aggression and die early and ugly like jungle creatures. We control those raw impulses. The fact that we name those impulses *nasty* is a part of our attempt to put a civilized lid on our worst selves. Marriage is part of that lid. It is intended to control our lusts, to allow order to exist in the community, to keep a man to his own wife and to leave his neighbor's alone. Sometimes this works but even sweet fortune-blessed King David couldn't do it.

Once we are married, whether a marriage began with love or as in other places on this globe today with social approval, or parental contract, the beast within us does not dissolve. We still want dominance or everything for ourselves. We still carry the ills of envy, hatred, desire for all the attention, goods, food, for ourselves. Male and female both would be willing at times to break the neck of the other. At least in part, at least a part of us is the soldier, rioter, looter, thug that you see on your TV screen creating so much havoc. Of course much of this is unconscious. We don't acknowledge to ourselves all the dark impulses we have. How could we live with our consciences if we did? But that doesn't mean that swimming about in the recesses of our minds, appearing now and then in our dreams, the demon we are does not appear and press us in odd and untoward ways. Jean Jacques Rousseau, the French philosopher of the eighteenth century who believed if we were educated properly we would all turn out good, nevertheless did describe, "that hideous sight, the human heart," and willy-nilly each of us marries one of those and brings one of our own into the marriage. We try to control our worst selves but things come up, things come out. We are not naturally all-loving souls. No wonder we need divorce.

Add to this our very human and universal fears and needs. Our fear of being humiliated, or abandoned, or unloved rides each of us in a different way, some more painfully than others. These fears make us test our mates, press against them too hard, demand too much, manipulate them or withdraw too quickly to protected isolated places. Remember that we were babies who would die if not tended, who had every right to fear another sibling's ascendancy, to fear a mother's love distracted and directed elsewhere. Remember that there is no human childhood without a record of insult and disappointment somewhere somehow and the present, the married life of an adult couple, becomes a place where these old feelings rise once again and infant battles are reenacted on a new stage.

Every child has had to leave the security of its parent and become a person in his or her own right. This is not so easy. We are all tempted to return to mommy and merge with her and give up the struggle of independence. At the same time we are afraid we will get what we wish for. We dread being smothered and incorporated by another. These are old childhood fears and explain things like the terrible twos and a child's fear of separation or difficulty in going to sleep at night. In marriage these fears are reawakened. We want to be our own selves not part of another. At the same time we want to let ourselves sink into the other and then may resist that impulse by being extra assertive or unpleasant. This need to be separate. This need to be close also becomes a problem in marriage.

It's no surprise that people can hardly stand being married.

And all these emotional minefields can make us angry. Often we are not angry at some specific thing a partner has or has not done. We all have inner climates that contain angry feelings that can be released at one time or other on a partner's head.

It's one of the wonders of the world that anyone can stay married and live happily in a long marriage.

What the Talmud Says

In the Talmud the Rabbis said that a man could get a divorce simply by serving notice to his wife. They also said that a woman could get a divorce if a man did not have intercourse with her as commanded at least once a week. Saying this the Rabbis (with sympathy for the female sex uncharacteristic in the cultures of the Middle East) made clear that a woman's satisfaction mattered and a man had obligations also. She was entitled to happiness in bed as well as the possibility of children. It touches me this. Think of it. Some Rabbi in the years before the first millennium was actually thinking of female needs and desires. Other Rabbis agreed. This ruling mutes the harshness of most of the rabbinical laws on divorce and reminds that at the center of marriage are simply two bodies with fierce needs and feelings ready to be wounded, healed, touched erotically and emotionally.

This ruling tells us that the idea of happiness in coupling, of mutual satisfaction, was planted deep in Judeo-Christian tradition. It didn't come with the Reformation, with the French Revolution, with the invention of the printing press. It was there in the small agricultural society of Palestine. The word *love* may not have been attached to it, but the concept was understood. A man and a woman should be content with each other and if they are not the man at least can do something about it. These ancient divorce laws were of course tilted most drastically to the advantage of the male. This bias followed civilization about as empires rose and fell. Even the ever decent and always far ahead of his time John Milton did not think of divorce as an option for women, rather as a tool for a man to right his unhappiness. He believed, as did all of his contemporaries and some of ours, that "man was made for God alone and woman was made for God in him." But all that is water under the bridge of American culture. Everything in life does not deserve a feminist reading. The no-fault divorce today is open equally to everyone. The guilty party and the innocent party (though there are rarely any innocent parties) are treated alike under the law.

Obsession

My first husband slept until noon, the shades pulled down. I went out to work. I had a job as a receptionist at a public relations firm. I lost papers. I misspelled names. But I could talk to clients so they kept me on. It was a nine-to-six job. It paid just enough money for us to live on if we didn't eat out or buy anything that wasn't crucial. He was writing. The purpose of our lives, the point of everything was what he was writing. He said he would die before becoming as old as Keats without achieving literary fame. I believed he would die if good fortune did not come knocking at our door. There was something in his eyes, in the way he would hide in the closet shaking a wire hanger in front of his face for hours at a time that made me think he would die. I assumed that I had been blessed with the task of keeping him alive, allowing his gift to flourish. I assumed that I was lucky to have been granted so serious a role in the world. I had a great desire to bring him happiness and satisfy the intense ambition he had to soar to the sky. It is hard to describe his wit and his beauty and my sense of privilege to be a part of his writing. He sent out stories. A rejection letter would cut him into little pieces. He would drink for hours and finally leave the apartment to wander the wilder streets of New

York, seeking comfort where he could. It was frightening to see him so undone, so unsure, so near to the death he kept promising. After one rejection from a prominent magazine he took all the monogrammed silverware that had been given to us on our marriage by a wealthy aunt of mine and went to a pawn shop. Every cent of the considerable money received went into a bartender's cash register. I didn't care about the silverware. I cared about the man. My stomach ached with fear for him. My eyes burned with worry and grief. I couldn't eat. I couldn't sleep. I couldn't bear how damaged, soul bleeding he was. I could feel his fear at being nothing, no one, as if his fear was gnawing at my own heart, was my fear. It was in a way. At the same time I thought to myself that if I were not playing this dangerous win-all or lose-all game with his fame and success what would I do? What would my life be about? Silverware?

Freedom, a Bitter Pill

It is true that marriage as an institution limits our freedom, but much as we in this country enjoy the rhetoric of that word, treasure it, have built our political system of which we are justly proud upon it, we know in the wake of the sixties carnival that total freedom in sexual matters leads to disruption of the home, chaos in the community, misery in the soul.

Freedom is a wonderful heart-raising ideal but not so helpful in the house.

Marriage is a way of controlling the errant human being who is ready to prowl the world like a beast of prey, taking what it wants, abandoning what it doesn't, leaving the bare bones of other creatures to rot in the sun. Once married we have voluntarily given up the freedom to follow our sexual desires wherever they may lead. We have given up the freedom to decide on our own where we will go on vacations, how we will spend our money. We have given up personal autonomy on matters as large as making new friends and as small as which brand of coffee we will drink, what television show we will watch. In marriage freedom turns into compromise which is altogether a less pleasant matter. We should be free from taxation without representation. Free from tyrants and slave drivers and censors and military oppression. We just can't be free from each other without being lonely. We can also be lonely if we are tied to somebody we wish to be free of. If God gets a second chance to design the human being perhaps He will correct this flaw.

You Can Always Get a Divorce, Can't You?

Today we tend to downplay the sanctity part of the wedding. The solemn swearing before God and community. We are used to hearing these words with fingers crossed. They have lost their binding power and are more like a sentimental nod in the direction of authorities: God and State.

Rather than hearing the rejoicing of angels most marrying couples feel as if they are part of a performance, a costume play put on for their families and friends, with all the best intentions of course but with a guaranteed out nevertheless, an out that would probably put a damper on the angels' song, turning it into something more like the high school chorus performing "It's a Small World After All" at graduation.

While the prospect of divorce is a sorry matter cheapening our relationship with a most serious ceremony it is also a life-saver, offering a second chance at happiness, and we couldn't live without it. Not now. Really not since 1643 when John Milton wrote in his tractate on divorce that "the pining of a sad spirit wedded to loneliness deserves to be freed." The Reformation had brought with it the idea of marriage as companionship, as a solace against the indifference of the world, as bringing to the married couple friendship, sexual love and peace. In the seventeenth century marriage was still the only place to have children but children were not the only reason to be or stay married. Social order of course was important, the caging of lusts was a good old Puritan idea, but added to it all was a new thought that people should and could strive for personal happiness. Milton said the laws forbidding divorce "hath changed the blessing of matrimony not seldom into a familiar and co-inhabiting mischief, at least into a drooping and disconsalte household captivitie, without refuge of redemption."

Well those of us who have been divorced and that includes 100 million Americans today know well that feeling of drooping and disconsolate captivity. This is not a trivial matter, not a headache that will pass. There may have been a brief time in the early seventies and late sixties when divorces seemed to occur more as a matter of fashion than fundamental necessity. But for the most part divorces occur because of disconsolate homes, because the companionship has ended, the solace has stopped and each of the partners feels isolated, separated, and lonely, frequently angry, and possibly one or other or both of them have begun seeking relief outside the marriage.

As a child raised in a home with warring but still wedded parents I am an advocate of the well-timed divorce. I am unconvinced by the argument that divorce is always bad for the children and that they will perform badly in school and life because of the divorce. Divorce is not good for children but neither is living with unhappy parents in an unhappy home. Children will struggle either way because they have endured a home with a noxious poison in the air, not because the parents freed themselves from their misery and found happier lives. If the parents do indeed right themselves and find partners that restore joy and peace to their souls then the children will at least spend some of their lives in a nourishing surround. This is not to underestimate the havoc of divorce and the difficulties that children in broken families experience. I want only to say that the trauma of divorce is sometimes better than the long-term ongoing trauma of living in a home with one or both parents dissatisfied and depressed. The ceilings of such a house seem low and press on the heads of the inhabitants and the windows seem always shaded from light.

Everyone decries the high divorce rates we now incur. Mainstream ministers, evangelicals, Jehovah's Witnesses, rabbis, priests, sociologists, talk-show hosts, psychologists, psychiatrists, and politicians agree. The crash endings of countless marriages are a sure signal that we are doing something wrong. We ought to have more marriages in better shape than we do but our incredible exploding divorce rates are also a sign that the ideal of personal happiness, of sexual fulfillment and emotional satisfaction, solace and companionship are alive and well. We are not cynical but rather over-hopeful. We have not, despite the dire predictions, become a society all bent on consuming, rat racing ahead, all four paws in constant greedy treadmill motion. We still want to love and be loved, and whatever that means to us at the center of our minds we notice when we lack love, affection, mutual companionship and we are determined not to suffer more than necessary from this deprivation. While every divorce represents a failure and is followed by a period of mourning and acute distress it nevertheless can be the beginning of things going right. There is something sweet and decent in this American hopefulness.

For God's Sake, Get a Divorce

When I was in high school I kept a calendar among my books and on that calendar I marked the days my parents had very serious fights and the days that they had milder unpleasant conversations and with a red pencil I starred the days that they turned to me and asked who started it, whose fault it was. I knew but I didn't want to say. I used a blue pencil to mark the days my mother lay in her bed smoking her Camels, drinking her scotch and covering her eyes with a towel filled with ice cubes in hopes of bringing down the swelling on her eyelids caused by tears, tears that she couldn't stop. I was trying to find a pattern so that I might figure a way to intervene, to stop the worst of it. My calendar was all marked up but no pattern could be found.

I am at Schraffts ice cream parlor with my mother and the year is 1945. Her eyes are hidden by dark glasses. She has cried all night. There is nothing new in this. I order a black and white soda. She orders a strawberry shake. She tells me that my father has betrayed her with a good friend of hers. She has found out because her sister saw them in the lobby of the Biltmore hotel holding hands. My mother is crying again when she tells me this. I am nine years old. This does not surprise me. We have been down this conversational road before. I pick at the scab on my knee from a roller skating mishap. It starts to bleed. I let the blood run down to my sock.

"Perhaps," I suggest, "you should get a divorce." Through my head a certain selfish vision runs. My father and I have a Sunday lunch, just the two of us. He would have to take me out to lunch once in a while I imagine. Also I want my mother to stop crying. Her face has collapsed in grief. People at the next table are looking at her. I am embarrassed. Again she tells me that if she were divorced all her friends would shun her. They would think she was after their husbands. She tells me she can't create a scandal. She tells me she is afraid no one would want her. I worry about that too. I try to comfort her. I light her cigarette for her. I drink my soda, what else is there to do? We have the same conversation over and over again for the next eighteen years. She has a trial separation when I go off to college but then she gives in and returns. What passes between them becomes a habit, a circle of promises broken, expectations unmet, and wearing to the bone. They were glued together by her money and his cruelty and her helplessness. I suppose one can become addicted to humiliation and accustomed to it and the dramas that ensue. As a child I saw an illustration of a dog and a cat fighting to the end in a nursery rhyme book. Pieces of each flew in the air until there was nothing left of either of them but patches strewn across the ground. For my sake my parents did not have to do this, for no child's sake does anyone have to do this.

There are many reasons why it is hard for people who should not live together to move apart. We tend to get caught in our unhappiness. He is cruel and she is the victim or the other way around and the suffering serves some inner unknown agenda of each partner. One is looking for punishment, the other to punish, and one is expiating old guilts and the other is expressing old angers and the result is a powerful magnetism that pulls the couple together against all reason and all odds. This sadomasochistic dance is performed with handcuffs on both partners and can go on and on for years. Since neither partner is clear as to what is the cause or nature of the grief they give each other, neither is able to escape.

The Ten Billion Good Reasons for a Divorce

There are divorces that occur because people are mismatched. Two fine souls just miscalculated. The charming man proves empty headed and irresponsible in the long run or the wife who has married him in the hopes he will take care of everything for her is disappointed or a beautiful woman turns out to have nothing to say and becomes boring as soon as the first blush of sexual excitement dims. She in turn is disappointed that she doesn't seem to please him anymore. Where once he hung on every word, now his eyes glaze over and he grows restless in her company. Then there are divorces that occur because one or the other of the partners is really unfit for marriage. A man who abuses a woman, a woman who is so depressed she can't fix dinner or hold a job or take care of the children, a man who is drunk before dinner or a woman who is frigid and paranoid and lives on tranquilizers or a man who turns his family into the target of his rage. Each divorce has its own story and each partner has a version to tell of his or her own and that version may or may not be accurate but it is sufficient because it is the story that is believed.

Sometimes we say, "What lovely people." "I don't understand why they couldn't make it." "They seemed like such a good couple." Indeed we don't know what subtle ways he put her down, or how she wouldn't let him touch her breasts or her hair. We don't know anything about the small details of living that go on in other people's houses and it is most often a misstep in these intimate matters that leads people to separate their hearts one from another resulting finally in the divorce, the one that comes as a complete surprise to their friends. Martin Amis said in his memoir, "In several senses marriages are secrets shared only by the principals."

One of the difficulties in thinking about the causes of unhappiness in marriage is that the language of psychotherapy seems gross and inadequate when we rely on it to explain the fine-tuning of intimate relationships. Interpretations and thoughts that are extremely insightful and helpful in the therapist's office seem brittle, dry and lifeless when spoken about in public, when applied to vast numbers of people, when used as catchall phrases. Novels and stories do better in describing our woes but the good ones sink into their own individual details: "He notices that she no longer has the nightmares that once woke her in terror and caused her to turn to him to hold her till the first light of dawn. Now she no longer falls asleep, instead watches television even when the screen turns grey and the picture is replaced by moving horizontal lines." These details are evocative, provocative, resonant if the work is good but they don't explain the drifting apart to us, not in a way that we can hold on to it, translate to our own lives, not in a way that would serve as warnings to us. Think of the thousands of *New Yorker* stories we have all read in which the epiphany involves one character or another recognizing the gaping chasm separating him or her from the love that was begun so promisingly. We see the truth in these stories and still we don't quite understand what happened. It seems almost as if a mysterious illness takes over modern man and causes disaffection, alienation, loneliness in the marriage bed. If it is an illness it is a plague whose causes remain vague and unexamined, and psychobabble only makes things worse giving us an expectation that we should understand the thing we cannot understand.

The End of Obsession

Sooner or later I was bound to see that art required devotion but not that much devotion. There was no real need for annihilating self-sacrifice on the part of the person tending the artist. There was no glory in doing so. The birth of the child I had wanted as a reward for working and supporting us while he wrote his first play and made his reputation forced me to see that our ties were thin. He was making passes at other women in front of me. He was leaving parties with other women while I went home alone. I was humiliated and furious. I was also aching with need for him. None of this is pretty. None of this makes me proud. All my emotions were in the service of a grand folly; to love more than one is loved is one of the great human catastrophes. Poor poor Swan, slave to Odette. Poor poor Emile Jennings who fell in love with Marlene Dietrich in *Blue Angel,* poor poor Meadow Soprano who loved Jackie Aprile more than she should have.

I waited for my husband's return in the small hours of the morning and with my fingers insistently drumming on the windowsill listened for the sound of his taxi in the street below. Hour after hour I watched the traffic lights change and the strip of sky above the avenue grow pale as the blue of an eye. I was worried about his safety. I loved him but my love was tarnished, bruised, turning bitter, and I was afraid for myself and the child. His wildness was far more than an affectation and I could see (any child could see) that his inner demons would bring us all to grief. No doubt the mad artist was more appealing in the abstract than in three dimensions in my own apartment. Up close this genius brought vomit to the bathroom floor, the shakes, betrayals of all kinds. I finally recognized that I could not cure what ailed him. I could not stop the inner gnawing of something fearful on his fragile spirit. When he moved out I was relieved but brokenhearted. I loved and hated him at the same time. He was also relieved. He had not liked playing house. Afterwards he did not come to visit his child. I was crushed by my error. Love died. But worry lived on. In truth in some corner of my mind I will always worry about him. I will always think of him as a falling star that shot across my life, brilliant lights streaking by. I had tried to find a man unlike my father. I had chosen an artist, a beatnik, a free spirit, a man of words not business. But in his indifference to our child, in his coldness, which was part terror, part ruthlessness, I had found again my father who had spent hours at his club perfecting his squash game while his wife waited dinner at home. I was running fast in circles.

I felt marked as a divorced woman. I felt ashamed of myself. I thought perhaps my life was over. I was twenty-seven years old.

Better a Root Canal Visit to the Dentist Than a Routine Divorce

Divorce is an act of violence to the soul and almost no one recovers easily from this blow. No one intentionally marries badly. Every bride and every groom has thought long and hard, as best as possible with only half the deck of cards in your hand.

Perhaps those men and women who have married six, seven, eight times shrug it off lightly, considering the financial arrangements as the most irritating part of the matter. These are people who keep hoping that in the next greener field something will happen to allow them to actually see, know and be known by another human being, one more handsome, richer, more beautiful, younger than the last. They drag their sorry selves from marriage to marriage the way an incurable cancer patient goes from doctor to doctor. But for those folks their trauma is not in the visit to the doctor but in the underlying disease.

Even when a short marriage ends it feels as if an amputation has occurred.

The divorce decree tells us that marriage is always a merger. Goods, property, status, and children are part of the deal. Who gets to keep the threshold and who gets the good china is a thing otherwise rational people can tie themselves up in knots about.

Determination is essential if divorce is to be avoided. You need some bottom-line belief that the family, the marriage, is not to be questioned, is not to be broken, is sacred and must be treated as such no matter what. For followers of church dogma this is easy. They may not imagine an alternative although I suspect that one lurks somewhere even in their minds in this modern world where divorce is as much a part of the social rules as the six outs in each inning of a baseball game. What is certain is that even the most religious and otherwise obedient members of the church may stray from their vows. The drive to be happy, the acute misery that a bad marriage will produce, can lead the most pious of people to separate, divorce, reconnect with another. Sexual attraction and temptation egg us on. One casual affair may be absorbed in most marriages but sooner or later infidelity will swallow a marriage whole. Like the transmission in a car that's been in an accident, the next bang may cause it to explode.

If the marriage is to hold, the belief in the unbreakable bond needs to be internal, not simply imposed by an outside authority. It needs to be a part of the way the couple view themselves and the world. The forever after part cannot be tentative, just until the weather turns, it must be absolute if the marriage is to have a chance for a long life. Even then there is a pressure point where determination to stay married for the sake of the marriage, for the sake of the children, for economic reasons, buckles under the urgent emotional need to separate, the drive for divorce.

No wonder guys like Donald Trump need prenups. They see the end in the beginning which increases the odds that there will be an end. It is true that the Jewish wedding way back in the days of the earliest rabbinic rulings included the Ketubah, the wedding contract. This Ketubah said nothing about love or honor; it was a practical contract about property exchanged. It assured the bride that should she be divorced she would retain the land, house, cow that had been her father's. Since she was unable herself to sell her husband's land the Ketubah allowed her to give up her legal claim to her husband's property if he or his relatives wanted to sell his possessions for her benefit at some later time. In other words, back when people were living in simple agricultural communities, when the great tomes of law were still small enough for a child to carry, the end of marriage was foreseen and the need for the prenup was clear. You can decorate the Ketubah with the most intricate of designs but you cannot hide its nonromantic purpose.

These days wealthy people draw up prenups hoping to protect their wealth from each other and their lawyers in the event that what starts out sweet turns sour. One wonders if the act of drawing up the contract distributing goods and funds prior to a marriage has any effect on bride and groom. It certainly sets off alarm bells. On the other hand why not have a prenup? Perhaps it will allow you to avoid the divorce courts. Romance is fine in its place but grown-ups face reality and reality is not just that marriages teeter and fall but that money and things are not beside the point at all and unmarried people don't live on thin air any more than married people. Married people often express their anger, wreak their revenge, seek recompense through material goods.

It is certainly without dignity or grace that people fight over their children, using them to harm the now hated parent. It is almost unbelievable the things that people are willing to do to their children in order to get every last dime, to humiliate or anguish the other side. This is not simple greed if greed is ever a simple emotion. What we see when Donna Hanover refuses to let her children meet Rudy Giuliani's lover or when Nicole Kidman threatens to take the children to Australia where they can be kept away from Tom Cruise, what we see when one society lady insists she needs $500,000 a year for her child's comfort or one lawyer spends expensive hours in court fighting over vases and rings and savings accounts, is an effort at symbolic restitution. If I can prevent you from having something or I can take more from you than has been taken from me I have not been damaged.

Revenge for betrayal. Revenge for disappointment. This is not strange. Who among us has never thirsted for a little bit of revenge?

If we think of divorce proceedings as something like arm wrestling between bleeding soldiers on the battlefield, then we see that like any other combat in which both parties have been wounded, dreams dashed, the petty and terrible squabbles that ensue are really an attempt to add strength to the diminished self and weaken the opponent. It is part rage and part fear that motivates these battles. Ugly as they are they do not so much measure our gross materialism as our capacity to confuse dollars with feeling, to imbue lifeless objects with powers that they simply do not have. Divorce lawyers benefit from our confusion between goods and love just as bakers benefit from our occasional tendency to confuse sweets with serenity.

Today divorce does not appear as a gross blemish but it still has broad economic and social consequences for both sexes. Today no one is socially ruined by a divorce but many are impoverished, their life savings halved, their homes sold, their children lost. A divorced man or woman is left with less—less property, less hopefulness about the future, less courage and less confidence—and it can take a considerable while for these things to be restored in good measure.

The chaos that we live with, the absence of social rules, the ease with which we may commit adultery or legally shed our partners seems not on the whole to have increased our happiness. We have our own problems which are themselves fodder for our novelists. As society has become more open and divorce more acceptable we are increasingly like dandelion wisps blown here and there with each malicious wind. Such a treacherous thing is progress.

Nevertheless I sing the praises of divorce. It is the valve that releases the bound from what Milton has called the "God forbidden loneliness" of marital unhappiness.

This is not a naive statement. I know perfectly well that the country is littered with lonely divorced men and women, more often than not women who cannot find other mates, who are struggling to raise children without a partner to bring in a paycheck, to hold a sick child's head over the toilet, to give to the child the advantage of a game of catch or an interest in marine life. I know that shuttling between two homes can make a child feel vulnerable, uncertain. I know that a family ripped apart can lose its home, its security, its hopefulness. There is nothing grand or beautiful to celebrate in divorce. It records a failure. Frequently it opens up a long hard period of struggle for both partners to reestablish their lives. Divorce is something you wouldn't wish on your worst enemy. Nevertheless we couldn't do without it. Every divorce tells us that someone hoped for something better in their lives. Without ashes how can the phoenix rise?

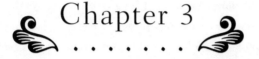

Chapter 3

Love—Oh, Please Don't Make Me Laugh

We are a nation that believes in romance. After all, we have a national holiday devoted to valentines and chocolate candy. Therefore when marriages go south we speak of love lost, romance withered. Love evaporated. It is true that holding on to love as Tom Stoppard said in his play *The Invention of Love* is like holding an ice cube in your fist. It will not remain an ice cube for long. *Love* is the word we give for the initial passionate erotic attraction, for tender feelings that may follow that attraction or exist independently of it. Love is the prize Western civilization gives us for losing our way in the woods, for having so many options and being responsible for our own bad decisions. Love is at least as old as the Bible. Didn't Jacob love Rachel, not Leah? Didn't Jonathan love David and David love Bathsheba? Personal affection for one's mate, either the dizzying kind or the more sedate, calmer sort of love, is considered an essential in Western marriage despite the ice cube in the fist effect, despite the fact that love at its highest pitch makes us blind, which is not such a good way to settle your affairs, commit yourself to a long walk down a winding mountain path with a particular person.

If you marry for love, as most Americans do, you are off on a wing and a prayer and you're lucky if you haven't been fooled into doing just what you didn't mean to do.

Emma Bovary and the Perils of Romantic Love

Emma Bovary, the main character of Gustave Flaubert's 1857 novel, was the daughter of a farmer in the north of France. She was convent bred and filled with a desire to experience the great enthrallments of love as she had learned of it through novels and religious teachings. She believed in beauty and transformation through love, but her image of love was mixed up with fine clothes, handsome carriages, money, and a passion that would never come down to earth, that kindled itself on secrets and desired the transportation of her soul to ever higher levels of sensual pleasure. Poor Emma was actually married to a country doctor who was neither very bright nor particularly ambitious. She soon realized he was not the love she was waiting for and began to betray him. This story has a sad ending, which might be considered a moral ending. She nearly dies of brain fever when one lover, Rudolphe, a wealthy local ruthless young man, breaks off with her on the eve of her elopement with him and she does die when the next lover, a young law clerk named Leon, proves unworthy of her devotion and she must face by herself the financial disaster caused by her borrowing and mortgaging to purchase fine items beyond the family means.

She lies and cheats and borrows money all to make these love affairs proceed. Disliking her husband, indifferent to her child, she finally steals arsenic from the local pharmacist and kills herself. She is the prime example of a woman who makes love and its erotic consequences the all-absorbing center of her life. The kind of excessive romantic heavy panting that she seeks is headed pell-mell for disaster because it is always based on misperceptions, illusions and delusions. Charles Bovary's love is not simply blind and dumb (although it has its sweetness) but also an illusion of his own construction. He never knows who his wife really is and when he finds out how she has betrayed him his will to live is gone and he dies of shock and grief.

What do we make of this now, a century and a half after it was written? Some express sympathy for Emma Bovary because she had dreams of a more refined and cultured life than the one she found herself in. Some are sympathetic to her yearnings for beautiful feelings, beautiful objects, higher society. We could see her as a victim of a social caste system, a victim of a patriarchal world in which sexual adventure was the only way a woman could adventure at all and sex was her only avenue of opportunity. But this view is too easy.

Emma is actually the voice of romantic love, missing the point of life, substituting shallow ideas for real emotions. She is incapable of real love, the kind that gets tested against adversity. She is scheming, manipulative and cruel to those who are most vulnerable, her husband and child. She does not need marital therapy. She needs a new soul, one that is stripped of the fashions of the time. She needs to get out of the emotional hot bath in which she has soaked so long that it has wrinkled her mind.

The Bovarys' marriage was by all measurements a catastrophe for all parties. In many ways the book remains the best indictment of the romantic sentiment ever written. But because we recognize as foolish, perhaps even evil, Emma's way of love, do we rethink our ideas about romance altogether? Is it better, wiser perhaps, to live without the heart pounding or racing because a particular person has rung the bell, is walking up the stairs, will soon enter the room?

Here is Shakespeare in *As You Like It*. His tart-tongued heroine Rosalind says, "Love is merely madness, and I tell you deserves as well a dark house and whip as madmen do: and the reason why they are not so punished and cured is that the lunacy is so ordinary that the whippers are in love too." This doesn't come as news to anyone who has been in love for sure. But wits and geniuses aside romantic love is now considered the sine qua non, the ground line for marriage. Romantic love is commingled with sexual desire and without it we now consider marriages fraudulent or at best "practical" and this word is said with a sad shake of the head as if one had ordered steak at a restaurant but instead received a plate of brussels sprouts. We believe in romantic love no less than did Emma. But we also have safety nets to catch the falling out of love. We have counseling sessions, retreats in the woods by the sea, conducted by ministers and rabbis and priests. We have marital therapists and individual therapists and advice columnists and support groups and TV talk shows. You'd have to be deaf and blind in this culture not to know that the initial love that begins a relationship is only the first baby step towards a union with roots deep in the ground, deep enough to withstand the storms to follow. Romantic love, candlelit dinners, intrigue, secrecy, passion, are just as dangerous for the harmony of the soul today as they were when Flaubert dissected them at his writer's desk. It is also just as tempting and perhaps just as inevitable now as then.

Emma Bovary is influenced by the novels she reads in which men carry off women into the night. She is influenced by theater and the opera and she confuses fine things that you can purchase with the real warmth of men toward women. Think if Emma had gone to the movies and seen Tom Cruise bending over Gwyneth Paltrow or Clark Gable whispering to Claudette Colbert. Think if Emma watched soap operas on daytime TV. She would have done herself in sooner, spun even faster to her doom. Our American culture celebrates the romantic all the time while confusing it with brand names written on the back of jeans. Our perfume ads alone produce Emma Bovarys by the truckload. Romantic dreams that depend on expensive accessories are particularly dangerous for the health and welfare of our young. Since Emma's day the situation has gotten a lot worse.

Boredom—What Does It to Us

One of the major perils of marriage is no peril in the usual sense at all but rather lies in the still waters, the shallow pool that marriage can become. If the same bird and the same frog come to drink at the edge of the pond day after day, and if the same weeds rustle in the same breeze the same way day after day, and the light changes morning to evening, winter to summer, the same way, season in and season out, and if the bugs lay eggs on the surface of the water and the bugs burst from larvae to wing and fly off season after season, same bugs, same larvae, same flight, then after a while it gets hard to notice the pond, to see the subtle colors as the dawn first comes. It gets hard to look at the pond at all and the eyes wander looking across the landscape for something unusual, something new. If any one of us were forced to live like a hermit, beside this pond, with this pond and its inhabitants as our companions, we would go lazy, still inside, unmoving, unexcited, dulled and dull like the still water, like the rock in the pond, slowly wearing away.

Ordinary life, the rising in the morning and the setting the coffee on its way and the picking up of the paper and the waiting for the bathroom and the sound of the neighbor's lawn mower or the doorman saying, "Good morning, nice day," are all part of the erosion of romance, the end of excitement, the dulling of the erotic factor. Children after the initial excitement of their birth can add to this drain, this dullness, this ordinariness. The game of catch, the pouring of the cereal, the changing of the diaper, the five hundredth reading of the same book, the day in and day out necessity of things, the trip to the supermarket, the loading of the car, the unloading of the car, the washing of the tub, the visit to the dentist, the daily work of doing for the family, the changing of the fish tank, the watering of the plants: this work, which is not arduous, is not unpleasant, is the building of the family, the making of the unit is dull.

A home does not appear with a sudden thunderclap of revelation, takes far longer than six days and arrives only through the doing of things daily, the phone calls, the arrangements for play dates, tutoring, eye doctors, the sweeping of the porch, the purchase of a flea collar for a dog, the wrapping of Saturday night leftovers and placing them in the freezer, repairing of oil burners, roller skates, washing machines. All this day-by-day work, this is the heat that makes the ice cube melt in the hand. Romance does not stay at high pitch in the course of streams of ordinary days and ordinary nights.

Here again Emma Bovary's tale speaks to the heart of the problem. She was a convent girl with a soul made for splendid passions, colorful moments, excitement of the grand romantic sort. Her life after she married the country doctor Charles quickly settled into routine, into dull conversation, into daily acts. She had little to do but watch the grocer close his store, the postman walk by the door, the storekeepers open and close their shops. Without outside excitement, without at least the pretense of passion, without something grand and beautiful before her eyes she became disconsolate, and her boredom spread across her days like a cancer threatening life itself.

In the era before one could live with a partner before marrying, the expectation of thrill at the sound of the doorbell and the arrival of the courting beloved was carried into marriage and disillusionment soon followed. The glorious intensity of romance is without doubt worn thin by ordinariness, by the sight of the toothbrush and the sanitary napkin and the sights and smells of real human bodies, well and sick, day in and day out. This ordinariness can be the death of a good idea, a marriage born in hope but never meant to be.

Now that many marriages are entered into only after some years of living together some of this testing has already begun before any vows are said and couples are entering marriage without some of the grand illusions for transporting happiness that plagued earlier marriages, that set Emma Bovary up for the calamities that followed. These days sex is hardly a surprise. If one partner or the other is unwilling or unable the fact will most likely not come to the couple like a sudden blow on the head.

John Ruskin, the famous nineteenth-century English art critic, married in his thirties a nineteen-year-old daughter of his friends. The marriage was unconsummated and seven years later the couple separated. Whether it was sexual repression, ignorance or reluctance that made this marriage fail one can't help wonder if a little premarital fooling around might not have avoided the calamity. When the English novelist George Eliot's supportive and loving partner, George Lewes, died, the novelist, then in her late fifties, began a flirtation with a literary man thirty years younger than she. They married and went on their honeymoon to Venice. On their wedding night, when he saw his wife waiting in bed for him, he jumped out of the window into the canal below, abruptly ending the marriage. These are stories of another time and another place when sex was dark and dirty and untalked about and religious repression was everywhere and many men had odd tastes that were not discussed at the dinner table or in the tabloids.

In this day of MTV and postcultural revolution, backlash and all, we do not in most parts of this country have so many virginal marriages and the genital nature of the other sex is less a final and majestic mystery than a fact of life easy to discover in a magazine at your corner drugstore. Sex today is not reserved for adults but available to many of those who have barely made it into puberty, never mind out of it. This doesn't mean that modern-day couples don't discover sexual problems along the way, only that they are rarely shocked or surprised by their mate's sexual habits, interests, desires.

But ordinariness, the dependability and sameness of gesture and touch, does indeed cut down on the erotic thrill of the encounter. If a man and woman have sex several times a week, maybe many times a week, sex does not lose its power to please, to bring them together, to provide physical pleasure but it does lose some of the deliciousness of the unexpected, the peculiar excitement of the newness of the other body, the way this particular body makes you feel. While of course sex and love combined is a very fine thing indeed, and sex in marriage can remain a pleasure for as long as sixty or seventy years, as long as the two human bodies survive, it will, no matter what the marriage manuals tell you, suffer from sameness and become therefore less thrilling. Which can in some marriages lead to bad trouble, to wandering, to temptation, to

seeking someone or something else new. Ordinariness makes
sex easy, familiarity makes sex wonderful and comforting and
good, but unfamiliarity has its strong inducements too.

In marriage these routines take on simultaneously a more
threatening and more comforting aspect than when two people are unmarried but living together. When the arrangement
has not yet been sanctified by state or church, and parents and
siblings have not been formally notified, and each partner
maintains a private bank account, there is always a sense of
testing, retreat possible, a threat of dissolution, a suitcase in
the closet that might be packed at any moment. This fact,
even in couples enjoying their time together, loving each other
deeply, headed toward a more permanent connection, makes
everything just a little more exciting, tentative, open-ended.
This is as true of the Sunday brunch at the local café as the
taking the dog to the vet or the way the fights are resolved.

Usually after a while one partner or the other begins to lead
the twosome toward marriage itself, and this creates its own
tension and hovers over vacation decisions, dinner parties,
questions as small as a new shower curtain or as large as a discussion of wanting or not wanting children. There are folks who
just don't believe in marriage on political grounds, feminist,
anarchist, socialist, bohemian, etc. They think they have just
removed the mumbo jumbo voodoo of the state or church from
their lives. But I think it's more complicated than that. They
may have one foot in total commitment to another but one foot
is not quite enough and the fears of being swallowed up by
another, absorbed into another, will not go away, creating a tug
and pull within the relationship. This non-marriage may be a

way to vaccinate oneself against the dullness of daily married life but it may also be a way of avoiding the richness within.

There are other kinds of familiarity besides sexual habits that pressure marriages, dulling the wits and lessening the electric current between the partners. His migraines, her incessant complaining about her mother or his mother, his loss of interest in his job, or her loss of interest in her job, which leads both to turn on the television set on arriving home and sit there without comment night after night. Her greater interest in the minutiae of her children's lives, who scored at the soccer game and who should not be taking ballet lessons, or his constant and all too familiar political opinions. Her fear of electricity which once seemed charming can become burdensome—his or her inability to balance the checkbook—all these repeated irritants in a marriage can become ordinary, not major problems, just like the rain on the pond, there from time to time, but cumulatively dangerous to the well-being of the marriage, to the freshness and realness of the partners' contact with each other. If whatever is happening day to day, night to night, is so familiar, can be grasped without the slightest effort at understanding or any struggle to accommodate the other, if everything has been done or said before, the heart of a marriage grows flaccid, the beat fainter.

We go to the movies, we watch television and on the screen there is nothing but drama, suspense, fear and resolution. Our own lives, which for the most part do not include spying on the enemy, catching ax murderers, saving lives in the ER, can seem sleepy, slow, dull in comparison. But this is the way it is in the real world. The dishes need to be washed even with a dishwasher night after night, the dog must be walked or the child away at college called or the one at home comforted through a nightmare. Routines have always been part of the human family. Even in the cave I suspect, the bones needed to be thrown out, the children fed, the fire lit or quenched, water fetched and each day required the same hunting, gathering acts, the same walk through the same path down and up. Since in those eras the life span was no more than thirty years or so there was clearly less time for the routines of life to grow tedious.

If you have ever been in a hospital for a major or minor reason and after some days you return to your own home you see the wonderful orange juice container in its regular place on the refrigerator shelf, you see the plant you have watered a million times on the windowsill, you see your old blue blanket and the cushion in the living room with the coffee stain. You relish the sight, you are delighted with the shape and the objects of your world and eager to care for them as always, to return to the familiar. Boredom drives us apart and threatens our marriages but at the same time we are blessed by the routine of things. Oh, paradox: you grab our human natures by the throat and sometimes it's so hard to breathe.

How to Keep Your Mate Interested

Over the long haul all the advice from magazines and sex therapists and talk-show gurus on how to keep your mate loyal and fixed on you just add to the noise pollution we all live with.

Losing that ten pounds, wearing sexy underwear, trying new positions, playing it cool or hot, taking a vacation without the kids, may be a good idea but it won't prevent aging from taking its toll, routine from taking its bite into your pleasure. No one has figured out how to keep all the daytime failures and stresses and exhaustions from getting into bed with you too. For most of us taking literally the dictum that you should never go to sleep mad would result in massive insomnia. People have been trying to suggest ways to keep attraction at a high enough pitch to serve as marital glue for a long time now. In 1727 Jonathan Swift, writing a letter to a young woman, Elizabeth Moore, on the occasion of her marriage, says, "The grand affair of your life is to gain and preserve the friendship of your husband." If we apply this sage if vague advice to males as well as females Swift would easily top our bestseller "how-to" list today.

He goes on to tell her a cautionary tale: "A pleasant gentleman said concerning a silly woman of quality that nothing would make her supportable but cutting off her head, for his ears were offended by her tongue and his nose by her hair and teeth." Sexism aside (given the absence of toothpaste and deodorant the fellow might have smelled bad too), Swift's concern about attention to cleanliness was sound advice for all times. Contemporary echoes of his wisdom may be no more than cynical attempts to sell us products that promise decent hygiene. A good bath may indeed be more effective than six months in marital therapy.

Swift was not a fan of female fashion. He informed the young bride that conversations about clothing were dull and remarked that "a petticoat will neither make you richer, handsomer or wiser than if it hung upon a peg." Which might imply that any old sackcloth will do and character is all that matters. This is a sentimentality we can safely ignore. There is some connection between sexual appetite and its outward expression. Our outsides are clues to our insides and our souls are only naked in dreary imaginations. What we wear and how we look and how we take care of ourselves is not beside the point, it just isn't the whole point. Some aspects of flirtation like small embers of the fire that once flared so bright will be fanned even in an old marriage, and a bright shirt, a shiny bracelet, a satin sheet may all suffice to send up sparks. While beauty fades and dowagers can't compete with debutantes and older men do not jump to arousal, the human sexual drive is ingenious enough, if not thwarted by misery, rage or disaffection, to find ways to remind, to tickle, to awaken the partner.

Love Patterns, Repetitions, Mazes and Other Games That Are No Fun

I knew two brothers whose immigrant mother loved them fiercely. But her mind had a dark and life-destroying cast. She was convinced her husband was cheating on her. She was convinced that the milkman was not giving her all the bottles of milk she was entitled to. She was sure that store owners shortchanged her. She was certain that neighbors were talking about her. She came to America as a seventeen-year-old girl without her mother and father and always missed them and the home she had left. She was melancholy and angry in some indefinable way at the losses she had endured in her passage to America. She was certain people were laughing at her. She was always sad and sometimes listless. It seemed as if a heavy cloud of worry and suspicion followed her everywhere. She smiled rarely. She was quick to accuse others of some crime against her. She was poor and hated her poverty; that too made her move with slow step and heavy heart.

Her boys grew up to be very different men, one from the other. The youngest became a lawyer and had a house in the suburbs. The oldest who had never been very good in school stayed in the old neighborhood, becoming a door-to-door salesman. The older brother married a beautiful woman, tall while his mother was short, a good dancer while his mother had never learned how, but after the birth of their first child this woman became seriously depressed and following on the depression she had a complete mental breakdown and was in and out of hospitals until she killed herself in her early forties.

The younger brother, a graduate of an ivy league law school, married later, shortly before his thirtieth birthday. His wife was a graduate of Smith College and when he met her a graduate student in sociology. She was studying with a famous sociologist who greatly admired her and expected her to have a brilliant future. She was a small woman like his mother but was sophisticated and worldly. She loved traveling in Europe. She played the piano and attended concerts of Mozart and Chopin at Carnegie Hall. The younger brother was deeply in love when he married her. He knew she had anxieties, was prone to make every decision a mighty matter that could take hours or days whether it was the purchase of a lamp or the right place for a summer vacation. He knew she was not calm or easy of soul but he thought that when they were married she would feel safe and comfortable and her worries would fade. In fact some years into their marriage she became dissatisfied with everything he did. She gave up her dissertation despite his encouragement. She grew angry at him over the smallest things. She grew suspicious of his affections and unable to prepare a dinner for friends so caught was she in a perfection- ist web of her own making. He too had married a woman with a severe and increasingly crippling blighted mind.

The two brothers, so different in their lives, were similar or practically identical in their choice of a woman, like their mother, with a disturbance of mind that would make life with them all but unbearable. They loved their wives when they married them. They chose them for their familiarity, similarity to their first love, their mother. They could not have known this. But love had lured them in exactly the direction they should not have gone. It is almost uncanny the way it happens, the way we re-create in the present the very things that stained our past.

You just never know, you never really know if the person you love is truly worthy of your affections or just a stand-in for some older pattern, some unfortunate primary mommy-daddy relationship in your life. Time reveals the answer. But we marry with risk, we marry the way a rock climber might put his foot on the next higher ledge, hopefully and with no alterna- tives in sight. When Titania falls in love with the ass due to some puckish mischief in *Midsummer's Night Dream,* she is duped by her emotions, unable to tell an ass from a fairy king. This mischief of course we usually do to ourselves as we fall in love and lose control of our judgment and marry in the heavy fog of one illusion or another. Love was personified in the classical world as the winged child Cupid wandering around with his sack of arrows. This image which has been transformed in modern times into the adorable cuteness of a valentine sent to a fifth-grade classmate nevertheless catches the ancient cruelty, the sharp point of the arrow, the randomness of its target, the indifferent playfulness of its intention. The idea of being shot with a sharp object is not how we might like to think of love. But the arrow which is usually restrained to the hunt or the battlefield is here used to convey the physical and mental assault that love brings in its wake. The lack of kindness, the lack of gentleness in this most turbulent of emotions and the vision of baby Cupid aiming his bow tells us exactly how childish an emotion love is, what a deep wound may follow.

My first marriage was with a man who no matter how hard I worked to ease his days would not cherish me. Many reasons. I was the wrong physical type. I was the wrong ethnic type. Perhaps at that time in his life no woman could have drawn him near. He was a wild thing, caught in his own desperate fears, somewhat as if I had taken home an antelope and expected it to sit quietly on the couch with me. In its panic the antelope would naturally rear and buck and dash out the door. So too my first husband. My father had married a woman whose body he did not like. He said so often. My mother had married a man who could not become her soul

mate or her friend. My father too seemed like a trapped animal when he was home. He roared and he bit at the hand that
was offering him food. My father had been from the wrong
side of the tracks. So too had my husband, although such a
different kind of a wrong side that I had not immediately recognized the similarity. Patterns are everywhere. They run from
generation to generation. They can bring good news or bad.
Our free choice in marriage partners is not as free a choice as
we might think.

The family therapists draw charts and show you in detail
how a strong woman marrying a weak man or the other way
around is repeated through the generations. They show you
how mothers and daughters, fathers and sons tend to do to
their spouses what was done to their parents, or repeat the
traumas of their childhoods with their own children. It seems
almost mystical this repetition of style, emotion, drama down
the years. In fact the way some therapists believe in this repetition is mystical or magical and perhaps a little overdone.
Other factors form us, other reasons for our choices are there.
Human beings are far too complicated to be reduced to flow-
charts however clever they may be. What can't be denied is
that the past hangs on. What we knew as children, the familiar
way, tends to sneak into our present life. There is something to
be said for always looking over your shoulder at what was
behind you. It may clear the path in front.

Most often human beings caught in marriages that make
them unhappy are not victims of their own bad values or
behaviors. The fault lies rather with the threads of their lives
which they have followed backwards into the Minotaur's

labyrinth in which they are trapped. The flesh is weak. The mind carries many burdens. Good people have real troubles.

Other Things That Can Go Wrong with Mr. or Mrs. Right

There are many ways to bring a marriage to its knees. A strong woman marries a weak man because she likes to be in charge and then after a while she doesn't anymore. A man marries a woman who is neat and clean and he admires that and then after a while he hates the way she picks up after him, the way she seems obsessed with dirt. A pretty woman turns out to be petty and mean. Something bad happens in the marriage like the sickness of a child or the loss of a job and a man withdraws from his wife, nursing his wounds. What if his business fails and he grows despondent and she feels contempt for him? What if she wants to see the world and he wants to stay home? What if he loves his mother better than her? What if she makes him feel inadequate or helpless like a child? The ice cube melts in a blink of an eye and what have you got left in your hand?

People do grow bored with each other, are incapable of loving when the bloom of youth is off. People do have needs that no one can satisfy and blame the restless loveless feeling that follows them everywhere on failures in their mate. There are a million reasons why marriages disappoint us but so often we waste our time looking at faults in the other when the mote is also in our own eye.

Sex: The Monkey Wrench, the Glue, the X-Factor

When Edith Wharton was about to marry Teddy Wharton she apprehensively asked her mother, what is marriage, what will happen to me? And her mother answered her with a tight-lipped, "That's a disgusting question," and that was all she knew about sex until her bridal night. We are led to believe that things did not go so well after that.

The refinements of civilization, the complicated rules of high society, were effective masks imposed on our animal natures. So much so that pleasurable sexual life itself had a hard time surviving the repression, ignorance, and denial that followed. It took Edith Wharton some fifteen years after marriage to uncover the erotic side of her nature.

As Freud's insights crossed the Atlantic and Benjamin Spock reached into our homes it became more likely that sex would be explained to a child long before the wedding ceremony not to mention the fact that in the 1960s premarital sex became as common as acne. Sexual repression and the hysterical symptoms that in the shadow of Queen Victoria were evoked in some patients became as rare as snow in July in most parts of the temperate world. The extreme reticence of Lucretia Jones, Edith Wharton's mother, with her unhealthy and unholy silence is gone but sex is still a thing apart from daily life, a place where the body can be renewed, where fantasy can fly, where the animal in us can romp. Or can't. Which sometimes still makes us sad and spreads disappointment through a marriage.

For a while there in the late sixties and early seventies everyone was talking about sex. You couldn't pick up a women's magazine without reading an article on orgasm, how to, when to and where to get therapy if you weren't. As the sexual revolution began (a personal side to the other freedoms that were erupting in the society), it seemed both shocking and pleasing that this most private part of our lives should suddenly be the subject of popular shows. Books appearing for laymen on our bestseller lists offered hope for a sexually happy life to every male and female entering puberty. Those were heady times and frankness was in, so were playboy bunnies and porno magazines, and while Jimmy Carter may have been lusting in his heart the rest of America was really panting and often in public.

Masters and Johnson working out of St. Louis were promising therapy that could bring sexual fulfillment to any dedicated couple. The shame and secrecy that had always made sexual pleasure so doubtful a matter were lifted and women were discovering pleasure spots in their vaginas and discussing this in their consciousness-raising groups. Marriages were breaking up because one or the other partner discovered that sex could be better than the sex they were having. If we could have a civil rights movement, we could have an anti-war movement, then too we could have a sexual liberation movement that would bring joy to our bodies, or increase our earthly share of satisfaction or so the drumbeat went. There were no ladies anymore and the double standard crumbled like a sand castle in the oncoming wave.

In 1972 the O'Neills, a pair of benighted psychologists, wrote a best-selling book they titled *The Open Marriage* and they claimed they had one and it worked. In the open marriage each partner is free to fool around with other people. They are allowed sexual adventures when they become possible. The idea sounded good to a generation that was breaking down the old prohibitions right and left. It fit right in with the rebellion against authority of church and state and school that was erupting everywhere. The book claimed that you didn't have to be a goody two-shoes to have a good marriage. And you should, in fact you owed it to yourself, to have a good time.

Several years after publication the O'Neills divorced. This was no surprise. First of all a lot of people were divorcing at the time, looking for truer, more authentic lives, fuller passions or just greener pastures. But besides the divorcing mania that seemed to have become epidemic the O'Neills discovered that infidelity in a marriage mattered. That even if you were open about your affairs and you had a mutual agreement with your wife, and the sauce was poured equally over the goose and the gander, some incalculable erosion followed on the infidelities. Recently there has been a spate of books suggesting that a marriage sabbatical or some form of institutionalized time off for good behavior would be a shot in the arm for your marriage. This is a rehash of an old idea that didn't work. Key parties from the heyday of the sexual revolution brought only chaos to the adventuring suburban couples who attended. Sex separated from relationship has a way of turning sour the next morning.

I was divorced when the sexual revolution hit my streets. This meant I could be free as a bird of paradise (not the flower—the bird) and taste of everything offered. It meant I could go out in the world and flash my colors around and would feel modern, with it, abreast of the wave. But there was a problem. My tries were all disastrous. I ended up crying or fleeing or locking myself in a bathroom. I had a child who had a baby sitter and was counting on my presence in my usual bed, by myself in the early hours of the dawn when she woke. And not only that, I could not imagine how to introduce her to partner after partner who would come through the door once, twice, no more. She was so hungry for a father, so hungry for things to be the same in her house, for order not disorder, that I could not play wildly, randomly, like a gazelle in the forest. I had already committed myself, before the sexual revolution came and changed the rules, bound myself into a sacred space where a child needed me to keep the chaos at bay, to find her a father for her to love.

Was I too much a product of my fifties upbringing or was I responding to something more elemental? As a mother I thought that freedom was a luxury I couldn't afford. I needed and my child needed order. Sexual connection plus love plus home is better for children (even if it isn't for parents) than playing in the fields of the Lord. Is this universally true? I doubt it. There are many cultures described to us by anthropologists in which men and women are parents and engaged in sexual dances with other members of the tribe. But it was true for me, a particular American woman, not so unconventional as she thought, afraid of breaking the most important trust of her life, that with her child.

The sexual revolution which was intended to bring us more freedom and expand our lives seems to have offended something in our souls that goes against the sharing of bodies, the passing of fluids all over the place, as if the customers in a crowded restaurant were to take a sip of their water and pass it on to someone at the next table. The sexual revolution was indeed an interesting idea, a reasonable reaction to the excessive secrecy and repression of earlier eras. However, except for the now common early sexual relationships before marriage that demolished the idealization of virginity and exposed the cruelty of double standards, the sexual revolution as it affected marriage itself has passed away, hardly lamented, an example of a basically sweet but naive hopefulness. It turns out that the monogamous structure of our society won't topple all that easily. At least in most parts of the world.

The conservative religious right is convinced that we are a society with lower standards than were to be found in Sodom and Gomorrah. If one considers where we were a mere fifty years ago and where we are now that view seems fair enough. Sex scandals occur all the time but today they amuse rather than scandalize. That the president had oral intercourse with an intern was not as shocking to most people as the opposition pretended. Today most of us take for granted an openness in sexual matters that was cause for giddy surprise and celebration in the sixties. What we are no longer talking about as intensely are the private matters of sexual function. While we have heard it all and know everything already, a certain shame plus a good deal of titillation has snuck back into the communal discussion of sex. Self-righteousness and prurience is such a delicious brew. Ask our Republican politicians who drank so deeply of the stuff.

The Clinton scandals may have been the last hurrah of the sexual revolution because we have come to see that there is an aspect of erotic mystery which seems to evaporate under too much talk of the mechanics of the thing. Like a belief in God some things can be overexamined, some bedroom doors need to be shut.

While pleasure is surely pleasurable, it didn't, all that orgasm-erection talk, in the long run make people feel much better about their lives, their marriages, their bodies.

Today men and women are still suffering from sexual anxiety. Sexual problems haven't gone away, they just aren't center stage anymore. They still worry people just as they have from time immemorial. Now they are less often caused by ignorance of the facts of copulation. There are sex ed. classes in almost every school. There are manuals and books and explanations to be found on the Internet and in your local bookstore. Unless you are home schooled you have heard it all ad nauseam. Nevertheless some of the same anxieties are hanging around. He wants to perform well, to give her pleasure. She is worried, will she respond well, will she have an orgasm? Is she pleasing him? Is she a healthy woman? Is he a healthy man? These performance questions still haunt so many sexual encounters and bring in their wake shame or disappointment or feelings of anger or inadequacy. The sales success of Viagra tells us that performance is unreliable. Women too have worries that seem to have dropped off prime-time TV but remained in the bedroom. The subject is still embarrassing. Why else all that "are you ready" stuff? Why else did we need an old war hero who was a political powerhouse in his day to make the pitch?

What remains wrong despite a certain clearing up of repressive shame is that sex is bound up in our souls with many other complicated feelings such as guilt and anger. Our unconscious minds run amok with secret forbidden desires and guilt about our illicit incestuous thoughts, or our destructive fantasies may hamper our sexual response. Our unconscious minds make childish, primitive mistakes and we are frightened of merging and losing ourselves in the body of another or harming the male or female who is our partner or being harmed by our sexual partners. We can be confused about our gender identities and uncomfortable with the physical realities that sexual intercourse presents. All those factors and many more can inhibit or destroy our pleasures. We all have sexual fantasies some of which may not be very nice and we may reject them and in so doing spoil our capacity for sexual response. Push away an unacceptable thought and the wiring may go dead. We may have trouble expressing just what pleases us, what would feed our fantasies. As a society we don't have the will or the means to offer every soul in-depth therapeutic work on their sexual natures. We simply don't know how to chase shame and anger away and bring pleasure to every bed.

In marriage sex loses its novelty. It can become routine or boring. But it can also be reassuring, exciting, a confirmation of the rightness of the couple with each other, their mutual respect and affection. Reproduction is a fine motive for sex but today marriage is intended for the long run not for the simple act of procreation. If the average family has 2.5 children the average person has a sexual drive that makes that number of occasions for intercourse totally insignificant. For procreation pure and simple we also have one-night stands or test tubes which do not require prenups or end in messy heartbreak.

The long period of human helplessness requires male and female to enjoy and accept each other's sexual natures, limitations and all, and get on with caring for their young. But sex can be withheld as a weapon against a partner in revenge for some other deed. Sex can be a desperate act to woo back a partner or an act of domination or masochistic submission. It can be humiliating or emboldening. It all depends on the moment, on the mood, on the particular marriage, on the fantasies of both partners, on the complexity of their story as they create it together. Marriage is then like a symphony in which sex is a major theme. It plays throughout, it goes slow or fast, it becomes dark or somber, it fades for a time and then reappears. It is heard in its silence. It is heard in its presence. Sexual problems are always marital problems but marital problems are not always sexual.

Isn't it nervy of us in this fragile new century to expect that when we turn naked in bed toward our partner we will be welcomed and our needs met and our offerings accepted easily? No matter how many times we have done the same things before with the same body, each time bears its own electricity and recharges our souls. Or so it should be and often is.

And sometimes it isn't. We haven't yet solved the problem of sexual malfunction, sexual boredom, the way sex and anger and sex and fear get caught up in the marital sheets. The politics of the matter are far less muddy, easier to talk about, than the specifics of each couple's private adjustment body to body over the years. The more you think about sex and marriage the more you see that we know little, can do little, are at the mercy of our earliest wiring. We do not see Prince Charming and Cinderella on to their honeymoon bed because all our fairy tales end at the altar. After that the plot grows too hard to follow.

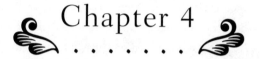

Chapter 4

Of Seven-Year Itches, Midlife Crises, Time's a Wasting

I am in Boca Raton inside a gated community. The houses are all sparkling white with red hibiscus bushes in the gardens. There is a golf course out the back door. There is a country club with a gym and personal trainers and a luncheon buffet with salads in silver bowls down the road. Many of the home-owners have retired. All of them have done well in this world. The sun shines down. You can hear the occasional grandchild playing in a nearby pool. This is the place, or not so many miles from it, where Ponce de León traveled to find the Fountain of Youth. The women married to the men in this community seem to have discovered the elixir all on their own. On closer look I realize that the women are on average twenty years or more younger than their husbands. They are with some exceptions second wives or maybe third wives. They have perfect skin which is well protected from the sun. Their hair is the color of spun honey. Their sandals have gold buckles. They have diamonds on their ears and their wrists and their fingers. Many of these women have also had surgery on their eyes on their chins on their lips. There is a certain tightness to the tissue that makes it hard to read their facial expressions. Was that a smile or just a quizzical thought that passed over? Their figures do not spread in matronly ease across the chairs. They too have done well and earned this life of leisure. But somewhere back in Chicago, L.A. or New York there is a woman who has raised the club members' children and her body like her former husband's will show the marks of age. Perhaps she too has married again. Perhaps not. The odds for her are not as good as for him as everyone knows. She needs a man at least her own age and that man is probably looking for someone still fertile, juicy, just out of childhood for his next bride. Her prospects are dim. His are just fine. This is not fair. But no one ever promised fairness.

I sit by the pool in my bathing suit and know that I am dowdy, frumpy, out of the game. I reach for the phone. I call my husband. He has a patient. He will call me back later. When he calls I ask, "Do you love me?" "What's wrong?" he says. "Nothing," I answer. "I'm old," I add. "What a surprise," he says.

In America we talk of the midlife crisis as if it were as inevitable as the terrible twos. Many marriages are said to collapse over this midlife crisis, especially the male version of it. It is said that men fearing the loss of their youth, the approach of death, need to reassure themselves of their virility with a younger woman who will bring them back to their earlier years, when all was possible and exuberance lasted all through the night. There is always the young assistant, the nurse, the librarian, the children's second-grade teacher, the accountant, the best friend's wife. Finding a partner to either fall in love with or simply amuse oneself with is not a real difficulty. Understanding what you are doing and why is a real difficulty.

We were convinced that herds of men were deserting fine women who had borne their children, suffered through the early years of their careers, shared their hopes and were now discarded like a tablecloth with too many wine spills upon it.

There is some terrible truth in this report. Men do marry younger and younger wives and start second or even third families. Saul Bellow had a baby at age eighty-three. Men with no hair and large paunches and ex-wives and married children are showing up at nursery school meetings in greater numbers than ever. These men have one thing in common. They can pay the tuition and a lot more as well. But how real is this? How common is this? This midlife crisis where a man buys a Porsche and a wife who looks like one too is probably as much of a fiction or rather a cartoon as any other stereotype: ditzy women who can't drive, soccer moms who haven't an idea in their heads, dumb blondes who are only after you for your diamonds, etc. These stereotypes exist but so do their opposites and a thousand varieties in between.

Yes there are parts of America where men buy beautiful young women who fill their closets with designer clothes and their hearts with nothing. Yes there are men and women who fear death and abandon otherwise reasonable spouses in search of the perfect orgasm, the perfect moment, the adventure they fear they will never have. There must be men who leave their homes and their children for reasons of vanity, restlessness, a grass greener on the other side, fantasy. But I'm not convinced that there are as many of these drifters and deserters as we were led to think.

Far more likely men and women alike as they reach their early forties or fifties may find the cracks in their marriage widening, the lack of affection they are feeling poisoning them, deadening them, depressing them. Far more likely looking forward to years ahead with the same sorrows as the years past provokes people to action, to leave, to start down new roads, to save themselves or so they hope from boredom, quarrels, isolation, unhappiness, their first mistakes which time has compounded and turned into grudges, resentments, lumps of coal in the Christmas stocking.

This falling in love with a younger woman, this running off to experiment, to join the boys at the bar, is usually not such a surprise as it may seem from the outside of the marriage. Something has been lacking, something has been winding down, something has been eating at the marriage for a long time before the eruption comes. It may well be that one or the other of the partners is incapable of participating in a living marriage but it is rarely mere or simple callowness that causes these separations. Scratch a man flying down the highway in his sports car with the beautiful lady by his side and you will find either a man with terrible limitations, damage in his soul, or a man who lived too long without the human connection he either craves and will one day find, or craves and will never be able to find.

We can say about these men that they have bad values. But that's only the outside read. It's very tempting to make that the only read. But I suspect that very few of the men on that golf course gladly and happily left their wives. I suspect that many of these men in their drive to make money lost their capacity for tender feelings, for understanding, for the moods and passions of their wives. I suspect that the culture of consuming which filled so many women's days may have left them brittle, hard, untender, unnoticing of the deep and constant male need for approval, appreciation, respect. In fact we don't know what happened before in any particular marriage. What we do know is that the bargain struck between the young wife and the older, wealthier man is just that—a bargain. Love or affection may be in the mix or it may not. This is a life arrangement and it is unlikely that the man will find what his heart desires and needs in this wife any more than he did in the first.

There is a sadness by that pool in Florida, a past with broken promises, a present with compromise and loneliness lurking behind the palms. This is not so much a problem of bad values as a more human problem of reaching another, holding on, enduring, actually knowing a member of the other sex in the biblical and other sense. It is not that these men should have behaved better (though some perhaps should have), but that things should have gone better for them. They were shortchanged of the best life has to offer and remain so. No need to envy them.

On the Side

Temptation is always there at the office, in your husband's best friend, in the car salesman, in the line at McDonald's, in the doctor's nurse or the doctor's person. Sure as rain there is always a new body bumping into yours, turning itself around for your glance. It really is a good deal to ask of weak mortal flesh that it bind itself to one person for a lifetime. That's why we need an entire commandment to remind us that the stakes are high and the game produces few winners.

I knew a beautiful shy young woman whose layer of baby fat had not yet disappeared who developed a crush on Mick Jagger. This was normal enough but in her college years she began hearing messages that he was sending directly to her as she listened to his songs on the radio. In these messages he was declaring his desire for her. This was the first sign of a psychosis that ruined her life. Her wish for his love passed into an unreal expectation and from there into voices in her head. Sexual desire was not the cause of her mental illness of course but it was central to her symptoms, central to her mind's disorganization. When the mind breaks down sexual fantasy runs riot and is restrained by neither religion nor reality. But when the mind is fine sexual fantasy is still there, like the theme music of a horror film, it returns with new encounters, new stages of life, and can cause damage to everything one holds dear.

It can be resisted as St. Augustine showed, it can be repressed as Freud explained. Jimmy Carter's "lust in the mind" was not so much a sign of his sinful soul as a demonstration of his quite ordinary humanity.

We are not apes who expect our mates to move from one to another copulating at will about the group. We are not dogs who come in heat and copulate with the first on the scene. For the civilized person raised from the first age of understanding to hide from others our bodies' most intimate places, vaginas, anuses, penises, and the acts of bowel and bladder, the personal private sharing of flesh and feeling that takes place between man and woman is simply so amazingly close, so raw, so separate an act from any other in our waking lives, terrifying in some ways, leaving us exposed, vulnerable that when a partner betrays the other even without breaking any God-given vows the robbed-of-dignity feeling that the abandoned partner experiences can be overwhelming: overwhelming is an understatement.

There are cultures where they say infidelity is not such a big deal. They say that in France and Israel a few affairs are only spice for the marriage itself, are shrugged off by the other mate, are not considered so fatal to trust and love as we in America experience it. Maybe this is so. There are cultures other than ours in which men are almost expected to have mistresses or whores who serve as mistresses on the side. Certainly Tony Soprano was raised in such a culture. So was his wife Carmela but his unfaithfulness still left a bitter scar right down the center of her marriage. Whether or not his sexual play was the cultural norm in her neighborhood, she was furious at him, unhappy in her own skin, and not the least bit accepting of his behavior. Perhaps this is because Carmela is not a first-generation Italian but has already been tainted with a variety of "only in America" dreams. But more likely it is hard

for all women wherever they are to absorb the idea of a husband's infidelity, harder than some are willing or able to admit.

Men of course for the most part find a betrayal by a woman
as a stab in the heart that they may never recover from. Some
men are patsies, wimps, desperate enough to take anything
the object of their desire dishes out. So are some women. But
these men too are hurt, really hurt, not just by society's
ridicule, which may not exist in our more urban anonymous
centers (when was the last time the expression *cuckold* sent
shivers down a man's spine?), but damaged in their own
pride, their own estimation of themselves, hurt in their virility, hurt in their potency, wounded oh so bitterly. O. J.
Simpson (that moral paragon) told a reporter that "if someone
fucked with his woman he would punch him out." Some cultures stone women to death for adultery. And they say Hell
hath no fury—. Fury is unisex. The papers carry a story every
few months of an ordinary man whose wife has left him for
another who gets a gun, kills her, himself, their children, her
mother, her sister: so deep is his hurt, such is the volcano of
anger when he feels abandoned by someone he needs, needs
perhaps to taunt, betray, knock about. Most men don't take to
the kitchen knife under those circumstances but rage they do
and drink and drive cars too fast and lie awake in their beds
thinking gory thoughts. Joseph Addison, the English essayist
writing on jealousy in the early 1700s, said, "If we consider
the effects of this passion, one would rather think it proceeded from an inveterate hatred than an excessive love."
Freud has explained it. The hatred comes from anger at the
person you need so much and has made you feel so vulnera-

ble. This tends to make a sticky package, one hard to put down and move on. Love one can leave behind, but hatred tends to nail us in place.

If Carmela had actually had an affair with her contractor or her priest and Tony found out about it he would have needed more than a psychiatrist. He would have fainted away permanently.

This matter of fidelity is the plot line for some of the best stories we have. When Jason dumps his wife Medea she becomes raving mad and kills his children in revenge. In some of the most celebrated novels we have, suicide and murder are two sides of one coin. Rage and despair fuel both. Despair always contains rage and rage is always permeated by despair. The proportions of that miserable cocktail tell us who will be alive at the end of the story and who will not. There are often forlorn children left behind, as well as a disapproving world. When Anna Karenina is finally crushed under the train wheels the tragic ending is both just and unjust. True she has defied the social order and so deserves her fate but on the other hand what a calamity, what a tragedy, what a travesty of justice it is to pay such a price for love. Even in our more liberal modern world when Michael Odatje portrays adultery in *The English Patient* both partners die terrible deaths. This is tragic but satisfyingly tragic the way great stories can be. When Othello just suspects that Desdemona has been flirting he kills her instantly. When Helen runs off with Paris the Trojan war begins. Helen took with her the honor of the Greeks. Many a woman has run off with a man's honor. Many a man has run off with a woman's pride, her dignity, her financial well-being in his suitcase. Without infidelity the tree of our literary tradition would be shrunk into a bonsai.

In the seventies I knew a woman whose husband, a prominent newspaperman with two little girls, began an affair with a newspaperwoman of much ambition and drive. The affair was not discreet. There were whispers everywhere. We were at a wedding reception with the original couple. The man had a glass of champagne in his hand. As he was talking his hand clenched the glass so hard he broke it, pieces of glass splintering, scattering about our feet. Blood spilled over his pants, across the floor. We picked up the pieces of glass. He returned to the party with a handkerchief soaked in blood wrapped over his hand. Soon after that he told his wife that he could no longer live with her and left his family for this other woman whom he married within a year. His former wife began a life of tranquilizers and psychiatrist visits and reeled around, half drugged, half furious, from event to event, lectures and movies, benefits and parties, with her speech slurred and slowed, her face crumpled with wounds. So bad did she seem that many people would avoid her, excuse themselves and turn away.

The fact is that in our culture to be rejected in favor of someone else, for romantic love to receive such a blow, is not really the bittersweet stuff of Nashville tunes. Rejection is not about achy breaky hearts, it is about real deep and permanent wounds that sometimes don't heal. Some people spend years walking around after midnight looking for their lost love stumbling, in danger of falling objects, speeding cars, fogged in, unable to rescue themselves.

In *The Scarlet Letter* society literally brands Hester Prynne with the letter A across her chest. This A for adultery is intended to humiliate her, to mark her as a social outcast, to prevent her from living within her small Puritan community. Hawthorne is not the voice of that community. He is its critic. It comes clear as we read the book that Hester is of fine and loving character, she is graceful and blessed in many ways. Her lover is the minister Dimmesdale who never acknowledges his role in her out-of-wedlock pregnancy, or even participates in her public ordeal. Her unpleasant and vengeful husband torments the minister who ultimately grows sick to death with his guilt. Hawthorne writing in 1850 observes the lack of humanity in our customs, the way we substitute obedience for life-giving emotions, how we confuse God with punishment, grace with conformity, love with sin. Some could say that Hester Prynne was a woman of bad values. But it seems more likely that the society in which she lived had bad values and she herself simply misplaced her trust, suffered from loneliness and had a soul far more glorious than those who judged her. Those members of Congress who sat on Clinton's impeachment committee speaking so loudly of character and values that they turned the country deaf are very like those citizens who were far further from God than they knew.

But what of infidelity leading to a new true love? What of all those men and women who married too young or simply badly, whose wives or husbands turned out to be depressed or mad, rageful or bitter, incompetent or cowardly, dull or inadequate in bed, with the children, or failures at work? What of all those who turn towards another out of deprivation, out of unhappiness, out of a need to escape? Infidelity can be the flip side of love, maybe even bring true and lasting love. One person's loss is another's gain. Sometimes infidelity is the key to unlocking the prison, the escape route through the tunnel, the way to retrieve happiness and all that is good in a good marriage. What if a man or woman finds his or her heart in flame, passions alive, hopes raised in the company of someone to whom they are not married? Common philandering is one thing but love outside the marriage is another, something worse.

Which is another good reason for divorce.

I know a man who was a successful business leader. Whose wife was quiet, dutiful, obedient, without sparkle or spice. There was something dry about her, uninterested in the world around her. She made you sigh when you passed her by. The man fell in love with an independent woman who owned an art gallery and introduced him to the modern masters. She was elegant, knowledgeable, and interested in music, politics, style. The businessman fell so in love with this woman who made him feel full of possibility and opened so many new doors for him to walk through that he wanted to divorce his wife and marry her. His children were grown, he felt he was entitled to the happiness that seemed within his grasp. His wife did not agree. She was afraid of being alone. She was horrified by the scandal then involved in divorce. She was not comforted by any amount of money he would settle on her. She said quite plainly that she would commit suicide right out of the window of their Park Avenue apartment if he left her for so much as a day.

The businessman was afraid she would do it. He was afraid he could not live with the guilt of her death. He was afraid that no happiness would ever be possible for him whatever he did. He stayed with his wife and gave up the love of his life. He lived a long time after that and was never eager to go home, always irritated and even rude to his wife, who lived fifty years more knowing that she had kept her husband through blackmail and that he truly loved another. This is a sad true story.

No one can blame him for staying. No one can really blame the wife for her terrible way of holding on. Everyone can regret that this marriage lasted and lasted its climate always one of regret and recrimination and loss.

Birds in cages are never beautiful.

In the New York psychoanalytic world there were two terrible scandals in which male psychoanalysts, both considered brilliant stars in their own right, broke the fundamental psychoanalytic taboo and fell in love with their patients. This is considered a colossal violation of medical ethics because the psychoanalyst has the absolute moral obligation to protect the patient from the fantasies he or she may have about the therapist's omnipotence. These fantasies are not based on real personal encounters. They are one-sided. Their usefulness lies in the fact that the transference of feelings from the past to the present onto the person of the analyst becomes visible to patient and therapist and can be examined. If the doctor responds to the transference as if it were love in the real world he no longer can help the patient understand his or her ways of loving and hating. Also the therapist cannot work with or aid a patient if his own emotions are clouding his vision. In psychoanalytic culture this off-the-couch relationship with the patient is considered as shocking and as evil as any other form of gross malpractice like operating on the wrong side of the brain.

The first psychoanalyst left his wife for a celebrity patient of great wit and humor. The day he told his wife he was leaving her she jumped out the window. Imagine how this doctor's other patients must have felt. Imagine the guilt that he must have experienced when his wife's great rage at him resulted in her death. He and his new wife moved away to another state but their marriage did not hold, perhaps it carried too heavy a burden. Perhaps he proved on a day-to-day basis less desirable than he had seemed as a distant therapist. Perhaps he was just too weary with his own regrets and the sting of his own conscience to sustain the hopefulness that marriage old or new requires.

The second psychoanalyst who fell in love with his patient and married her left behind an angry wife and angry children. This too created a major scandal in the psychoanalytic community. The taboo had been broken again. The wife recovered and remarried but the psychoanalyst now in a marriage with his patient was having serious trouble. The couple moved away and attempted to begin again in a place where the story of their doubly illicit relationship would not be so interesting to others in the community. The psychoanalyst, who had successfully battled a depression of his own all those past years, now became increasingly melancholic. As his second marriage was showing severe signs of strain, perhaps his new wife was intending to leave him, he killed himself. Ah, what a morality tale this was. Fall in love with your patient, act on that love and you die or someone dies.

Folk wisdom, that which we imbibe with our mother's milk, tells us that men have a more powerful sexual drive than women and they need sexual activity more often than women. It is true that when men were beasts literally, not figuratively, they may have spread their seed across the available females in reasonable hope of increasing the odds of genetic success. But if they didn't stick around and help the female protect the helpless child their DNA was toast anyway. So while we hear of men who need many women, wives, mistresses, concubines, interns, students, etc., we cannot assume that this is a pure genetic environmentally favored physical drive, one too powerful to submit to the required social controls.

If it is simply in the male character, a given, then we must be understanding and forgiving of men who are always looking for an additional roll in the proverbial hay, even if the hay is the carpet of the Oval Office. But sexual drive in human beings is always caught in the psychological design of our beings. It can be used to help us escape love or closeness or responsibility. It can be a disguise for contempt for women, reducing them all to whores. It can be an expression of anger at a particular wife who withholds warmth or belittles the man's accomplishments. This vaunted male sexual drive, the constant seduction process some men act out, can be a cover for their fear of ineptness, sexual weakness. There are so many reasons a man thinks he needs to have his way with any attractive female in his purview that it seems naive to believe he was just born that way.

Our society with its harsh patriarchy and its custom of greater male freedom and female restriction has created an illusion that the double standard suits our nature. It doesn't. It suits some men some of the time, and not for reasons that in America today make them happy or signal their true masculinity.

Why Infidelity Is a Mortal Wound

Aside from religious edicts what really is so compromising about infidelity that it threatens a marriage and is the immediate presenting cause of so many divorces? Yes, it breaks the physical intimacy of the two partners and introduces a third person, but aside from matters of pride (why wasn't I enough?) there is something even more horrible and dangerous about the event that lurks just behind our conscious thoughts. It has I think to do with the way we attach ourselves in marriage to our mates. That attachment is a grown-up version of our primary and first love of our mothers. The baby needs its mother or it will die. The baby fears abandonment above all else. Listen to the blood-curdling shrieks and the heartbroken sobs of an eighteen month old as the parent leaves the home, never mind that a competent baby sitter is in charge. We must trust that our parents will feed us—protect us from fire, cold, drowning, loneliness—and are bonded to us above all others. That need is so great and fundamental that it casts a strange shadow over the rest of our human lives.

In marriage we of course have mutual responsibilities. We may at times play the part of the baby and at other times of the adult but in general we know we are both in one person and we give and receive tenderness, care, protection as the moment arises. But if one partner has deserted the other, turned to a third person, if only on the third Tuesday of last month and the month before, then the fear that shakes the relationship is deep, indeed as deep as our earliest infancy, and awakens our primitive fear of abandonment.

When siblings are born, or when the youngest child recognizes that there are others before him, the disillusionment that follows is bitter to swallow. We want the exclusive love of our mothers. We want this because we know how helpless we are without them. We know that our rivals may take her attention away and we fear we may be harmed without her constant care. This is a small child's vision but it hangs on—it affects us as adults. It makes this matter of exclusiveness all-important. The person I have this extraordinary closeness with, who sees my body, who touches my private areas, who gives pleasure, who is everything to me, must love only me, touch only me, or I will be in danger. This is not such a rational thought. No physical danger follows on adultery. Yes, there is the possibility of disease but the kind of fear we see is provoked not by actual reality but by an old psychic experience and pulls us back to our most vulnerable earliest infant experiences when we first discovered that we needed desperately and were dependent on another's ministrations.

Along with the fear of abandonment the child experiences anger, anger at the very mother he or she most needs. So the partner in a marriage who has been betrayed becomes angry, perhaps angrier than ever before in his or her conscious life.

This rage is reasonable enough. After all a real-world betrayal has taken place, a vow has been broken. But the rage also carries ancient rages, not so reasonable, provoked by the present situation but not of it, old feelings about older disappointments in the mother-child time.

Dear Lord, Don't Let Me Be a Movie Star. . .

Hollywood is a place where the divorce rate has reached one out of every one marriage. This doesn't mean every last marriage ends in divorce but that some people are divorcing many times and in any given year there may be as many divorces as there are marriages. In addition, as anyone who has stood in a checkout line at the supermarket knows there is a constant change of partners among movie stars, who appear like the common bee to be programmed by nature to go from flower to flower, a crew of drone paparazzi following their erratic flights. Unlike bees they do this for their own pleasures, returning to no hive and submitting to no monarch. Since they can buy anything they want they are not anchored to reality as are the rest of us. They have no need to temper their impulses, stifle their instincts. They can have pretty much what they want. They appear to have more opportunity and freedom than the rest of us mere mortals.

They are for the most part particularly beautiful and charismatic people who are always sending out vibes, "love me," "adore me," "admire me." That is in the nature of the star. We don't know exactly what creates this "you can't take your eyes off me" quality but it seems rarely to be an excess of confidence, a childhood of comfort and pleasure with all the necessary ingredients nailed into place for a self that can survive in solitude, that thrives without external approval. Each of these flitting stars has their own reasons, their own stories that they tell again and again to their therapists, to their scientology mates, to their astrologers, masseuses, personal trainers, nutritionists, channelers, chauffeurs, etc.

It is the job of the tabloid press to ferret out these sad tales and couple them with pictures of the latest amour, the newest scandal, the infidelity du jour, to tickle and amuse and satisfy the hungry public, hungry not just for visions of the life of the stars but for a sign that they have human troubles, failures, just as if they weren't stars.

What could be more interesting than the fact that so-and-so has entered a drug rehab facility or that so-and-so reveals that she was molested as a child by a drunken father or that such and such a married man is really gay and has a secret lover up in the hills of Malibu? It is never unpleasant to learn that folks with so much money, so much success at their fingertips, are after all only mortal and fall hard on hard times of their own making. That fact suits our sense of justice, eases our envy and makes us feel closer than ever to our celluloid friends, whose names we know when they don't know ours.

The stories of the Greek gods and goddesses served as entertainment in a time before the printing press or Barbara Walters. The Greek gods had very human faults, infidelity being one of them. Zeus is forever betraying Hera who roves the world looking to take revenge on the objects of his love. She is reported to have turned rivals into cows or swans. These stories served to bring the Greeks closer to those who had power over them. They served to explain the less than ideal moral failures that mar human life. If even a god could cheat on his spouse why not a mere mortal? Our firmament today is inhabited by movie stars, top-of-the-charts musicians, and athletes all in perpetual sexual motion.

The movie stars because of their work on distant sets have forced separations from their mates of many months at a time. During the shooting of a film they will naturally become close to any number of other people including costars. They are play-acting at love with strangers and it is hard to keep the playacting just pretend. Sometimes it slips into reality, or is it always playacting even when no director is present at the scene? They are used to instant gratification. Why not have this other body if it is offered to me? They also have a sense of being special, above the rules, so outstanding and fortunate that they are not required to bend to the disciplines that the rest of us endure.

Which means that they are tempted into infidelity by their own need to test their lovableness, their seductive powers again and again, after all that is what they do for a living. They are also tempted by the lack of communal disapproval, the fact that romance is expected of them, that they are not enhanced in their glamour by faithfulness or signs of ordinary life. There are no scarlet letters sold on Rodeo Drive. Actors and actresses also may have a shifting, shaky sense of identity. Their needy souls may require reinforcing through new conquests and fresh stirring of emotion, just to prove they are real, really here, really all right. Being self-obsessed doesn't mean that you feel better about yourself than others. It likely means you feel worse. Narcissus needed admiration so much he drowned in his own reflection or so the story goes.

When non–movie stars commit adultery some of the same motives may be at work. We too may need to prove our attractiveness, our acceptability, our lovableness again and again. We too, even without unlimited funds, may not be sure who or what we are or should be and find ourselves most really alive in the pursuit of another. We too may feel entitled to more than we have, to taste everything as if we were a god on the top of Mt. Olympus or at least to carry on as if it were so. And of course we too may look in the mirror and see no reflection, feel ourselves hollow, empty, and not real, not really there. We too may reach for another body to reassure us. Take the Toyota salesman Henry Angstrom, known to all as Rabbit, the hero of John Updike's quadra-headed novel. We see him scan every woman passing as if she were a sexual possibility and when one comes by that will have him he falls into bed, a thrashing of limbs, a temporary easing of the pressure, but then again and again he finds sexual conquest the wrong cure for what ails, which is a pervasive and totally incurable sense of loneliness.

When Tony Soprano has sex with one of his ultimately demanding mistresses he is distracting himself, playing just as he does in his strip club with women as baby dolls, women as objects of physical pleasure, as distractions to the tensions of the day. The problem for Tony is that women, his sexual partners, have voices of their own and wishes and demands for time and presents and attention. The Madonna-whore split exists in his head not theirs. This is not what he wanted or bargained for. His ladies of the night have great holes in their hearts and weep and scream and throw things about. They don't provide what he needs. Maybe his mother should have done it? Maybe his wife would if he could let her? The problem with Tony's infidelity is that like most people's bid for freedom it only locks him into himself, double locks, triple locks, doors closing. Not jail (in his case also a possibility), but just his life.

We tend to think of celebrity infidelity as a game they are entitled to play for our amusement. We tend to scold them for thoughtless behavior and blame it on the excess of money and the by-products of fame or the power it seems to put in the hands of the holder. But actually those who seem powerful are often merely frightened of losing everything, afraid of being exposed as frauds, afraid of the dark like everyone else. We know this was true of Marilyn Monroe. We know this is true of many stars whose actual lives are wrecked by inconstancies of their own and others.

The family values preachers can speak about Hollywood as if it were Sodom and Gomorrah but that split is too easy. The mote is in all of our eyes. We do not upend our marriages, leave our children, drink too much or gamble away the rent money because Hollywood showed us how. Our movie stars and sports stars echo our own confusions, not the other way around. The family values types who wish to turn back the clock forget that the sexual revolution merely made open what had previously been secret. It did not destroy happy homes or afflict peaceful simple souls with unrest. Incest, desertion, pornography, prostitution, drug abuse, battered women, alcoholism, single-parent homes, all existed long before the Playboy bunny, long before Betty Friedan, long before the X-rated movie and *People* magazine. To live with constancy and love, to face all difficulties together, not losing one's partner or one's mind, is not so simple a matter and we cannot be commanded to do so, nor can we rein in our lust or our need so easily, not for God, not even for our own children's sake.

. . . Or a Politician

Some men and some women just have infidelity ticks as hard to control as the kind that pulls on the eye muscles or makes the head turn right or left at odd moments. There is no question that our Bill Clinton is such a man. He was always charming people, he was always seducing them usually for their vote or so it was before he became a former, an ex, an out-of-work politician. This seemed quite normal for a person seeking higher office. In fact it may be a requirement. This desire to be loved by the anonymous public as they vote in secret on election day can so easily become literal, rather than metaphorical. Sexual favors, sexual indulgences can be the effluvia of the energy of the endless seduction of the public that marks the political process. Sex appeal, sexual oozings are part of the courtship of many politicians, most successful ones, as they travel the country shaking hands and looking people in the eye. Sexual vibrations come off some politicians in the same way they come off rock stars, as exaggerated, palpable, audible vibrations in the air. They have an aura of sexual magic following them about from one fundraising chicken dinner to the next. Think of John F. Kennedy, who was considered one of the great playboys of all time. Think of Nelson Rockefeller dying in the bed of his mistress.

The problem for Bill Clinton was that his rather outsized sexual appetite needed continual appeasing. He was interested in women unlike his wife, inferior in education, in status, in cleverness. He was interested in sex with wrong-side-of-the-tracks women like Paula Jones. He was interested in interns with baby fat still on their bones. He was attracted not to brilliant women who might offer him intellectual companionship and challenge. Instead, like a high school boy he wanted the girl who might put out, the one he might get to home base with. "Aw, grow up," one wants to say to him. But he is not alone in his tastes. All over the country there are men who have respectable wives who are their equals in class, education, profession but who on the side keep the other kind of woman, the bad girl, the girl from the wrong side of the tracks, the girl you can't bring home to mother. Whatever else the man is doing with this split, one that separates real life with real sex pitting nice vs. not-so-nice girl against each other, it is no compliment to either woman. Some men are just unable to place sex and love together in one body. Too much guilt, too much talk of sin has created a big problem.

The Clinton kind of sexual philandering reveals a culture that makes women into creatures they are not and leaves men without true erotic companionship. What they lose is eros combined with love. What they have is eros reduced to late-night porn. In repressive, sexually inhibited cultures where sex is equated with sin and pleasure, sensuality itself is of the devil's making, men may think of sex as something dirty, something nasty, something that gives them joy yes, but illicit joy, bad joy. They split their relationship to women into two parts, the nice and the dirty. The dirty they keep away from their wives. (Tony Soprano too.) Problem is that the dirty is where the pleasure is greatest and the temptation highest and so as they betray their wives they keep them clean but not quite loved, not fully loved. Sex and guilt become accustomed to each other, wrapped up as they are in the sin package. This Madonna-whore solution compromises everyone involved. The fires of hell may await sexual sinners but labeling masturbation and sexual thoughts as sins has not made it easier for humans to be faithful and may be as counter to real family connections as the porn magazines hidden in the sock drawer.

The kind of infidelity that Bill indulged in is far less threatening to a marriage than the kind that Franklin D. Roosevelt enjoyed for many years. Roosevelt had a lover whom he held dear and who became an important part of his days and nights bringing him consolation and joy and companionship in a way that his wife, wonderful as she seemed to much of America, could not. That extramarital love was a real violation of marriage, not a playful thing at all, not a one-night amusement in the Oval Office but a true relationship with a home and a history and a memory of its own. If presidents could have divorced in those days perhaps the Roosevelts might have divorced.

There was much talk of character in the 2000 presidential campaign. Republican and Democratic candidates alike bent over backwards to assure the American public that they were men of character, which was a code word way of saying they wouldn't be caught with their pants down with an intern, because they were good men who were faithful to their wives. The candidates seemed to be telling the truth about their commitment to the laws of religion but they ended up contributing to the atmosphere of hypocrisy that covers so much in American life. Infidelity (or what the Bush team would call bad "character") cannot be the determining factor in whether or not a particular man will make the right president for our country at any given time. No one takes that idea seriously. Almost all of our past presidents have dallied outside their marriages. Character or at least the kind we need in our leaders is not so much tested in the crucible of marital relations as in their fidelity to the positions they have staked out, to our laws, their sense of obligation to the vulnerable among us, to our economic and social well-being, to peace in the world, to human rights about the globe.

The bad boy behavior of some of our politicians fuels the general impression that America is on its way to damnation but our general forgiveness of sin in famous places is not a sign of our corruption, rather it speaks well of our collective wisdom. We all know that it is hard, very hard, for ordinary people to live in long-term relationships. They often fail. How can we ask of our much-tempted stars and our politicians that they both seduce us constantly and also provide us with role models of sacrifice and sanctity? That's not their job. It is probably as pointless and irrelevant to ask of politicians that they remain faithful to one partner as it is to ask movie stars or rock stars to keep their hands off other people's mates. For the rest of us our personal decisions are personal.

Guilt, or Paying the Piper, Whomever He May Be

Emma Bovary and Anna Karenina, women who both betray their husbands, are punished by the authors as they turn to suicide as their only way out of a hopeless situation. In our stories the adulterer's transgression often leads to a tragic resolution, which we as readers in search of moral order seem to require. In Graham Greene's *The End of the Affair,* the woman gives up the man because she can't break her vows to God whom she believes has in answer to her prayer created a miracle and saved the life of her lover. She becomes fatally ill and dies reconciled to God but without the great love of her life. This seems a fair exchange to some people, Graham Greene for one. I would worry that this might be an empty gesture towards an unlistening God who is not so interested in my private sins considering the very major ones that cause destruction all over the earth. It is very hard for a modern person to sacrifice so much for the rules of a God who may or may not exist. God has kept his face invisible while man has committed such havoc on man as we have seen in this century. There were no major miracles in Auschwitz, no trains mysteriously stalled on the tracks, no blockage of the gas pipes that fed the crematoriums, no miracles at Verdun, in Cambodia, in My Lai, in Rwanda, in the Sudan, in Stalin's Gulag, no miracles at all. So it does make one wonder if God noticed that Emma Bovary was carrying on with Leon or that Anna was in love with a man she was not married to. But we have noticed and the plot lines of our great books seem to give us again and again the moral justice we require while at the same time allowing us to imagine the excitement and temporary bliss of betrayal.

There are religious folk who do not question God's law and if their marriages had died at the roots they would still stay with them till death do them part, out of a sense of duty, obligation, a profound belief in the morality of their sacrifice and the power of their vows. I regard this honorableness with mixed feeling. Yes, it is upstanding. Yes, it makes possible an ordered society where people behave and stay in the place they have put themselves. But how ghastly is the loss of opportunity for real human affection. How terrible it is to be condemned to dinner, to walks, to conversation, to the bed, of a person no longer respected, desired, chosen, inferior to the real or imagined other more loved one. To live this way seems anti-life, anti-all that is song within us.

Many infidelities are not whimsical impulsive acts but come out of a struggle to save oneself from a forlorn or painful marriage. It is hard to be against the love of man and woman when it is true and fierce and fills the two with new hope for themselves and their progeny. The rules of society can't be treated like a card game in which cheaters if they have fast hands may get away with aces up their sleeves. But maybe

there are circumstances, reasons, justifications for some infidelities. Perhaps everybody need not sacrifice their personal
happiness for the rules. Clearly many people can't and don't.
Most of us cannot lean back on the absolutes of a church as it
interprets God's will. Some of us would think that same God
might want us to love and be loved and to have the courage to
undo a mistake and try again. We can speak then of infidelity
as a sin or we can speak of infidelity as spark of hope, a kind of
prayer of its own which it may also be.

Some would not worry about God's opinion but might
grieve to the bone over the pain that their children suffered if
a marriage breaks and moon like guilty ghosts about their children's lives ever after. If the children begin to show signs of
inner disorder, sleep disturbances, regression to wetting or
thumb sucking or end up with school problems, aggression
problems, delinquency, promiscuity, fearfulness, timidity, all
the things that can and do appear in the unhappy child (actually with or without a divorce in the family), a parent will haul
himself or herself over the coals, feeling responsible for the
shaky ground on which their children were forced to pitch
their tents. The anxiety over the children, the guilt one feels
towards them makes it hard to parent them in whatever portion
of time one has and it places a terrible pressure on the new
partner and the new marriage. Children will see their parents
as engaged in a species of horrid infidelity when they find new
partners. We may believe in divorce, divorce may be legal but
for the child the new partner is always a result of infidelity to
the former husband or wife and as such is hard to swallow,
hard to accept.

Guilt is a burden that makes us do unpleasant things to ourselves. A person who feels at odds with his or her conscience can hardly enjoy whatever lies before him. Most of us do live with guilt as a bad companion, a heckler, a spoiler, an invisible hand that leads us down roads we ought not to go. Infidelity of any kind increases the pot of guilt within until it may overflow and ruin everything.

Am I the Oldest Living Monogamist?

In 1973 as the new sexual freedoms were becoming commonplace, sweeping through middle-class homes such as ours, a sixteen-year-old teenager in my family turned to me in irritation one summer, a summer she was spending on the beach with boys and at late-night parties in the dunes (where what I was worrying about happening was happening), and said (in that tone of voice teenagers can use that produces in the listener the desire to grind the teeth), "You and Dad are the only people on the face of this planet who believe in fidelity anymore. You're so out of date." This stung. I had thought of myself as a revolutionary, a lover of freedom, a rebel against conventional bonds. I had worn black leotards in college long before this became the emblem of the new generation. I had engaged in premarital sex when my mother believed with all her soul that a loss of virginity would make me unmarriageable and condemn me to a life of single misery. I risked it. I had been ahead of my times, never a sheep that followed instructions. Nevertheless this teenager had a point. Now with a family I had become less of an adventurer and it was true I did value fidelity, not in the abstract but in the most particular, mine to him, his to me.

When I met my husband he was already divorced. I was a single mother. So I was surprised that after our first date which was on a Friday night he called and invited me out for the following Friday. I was surprised that after a month of Friday night dates he seemed not to want to come upstairs with me. Perhaps he was gay. Perhaps he was really married and I had been completely fooled. Perhaps he had problems. I had dated enough to know that all of the above could have been true. I knew that sex was not so simple for men as it might seem. I also knew I was listening for his voice, remembering his smile all through the week. Perhaps I should stop seeing him before I became so attached that a break would knock me down, bury me under a mountain of disappointment.

A few weeks later I asked him why he only saw me Friday nights. I was too shy to ask about why he hadn't even begun to approach any further intimate activity, though I could feel him wanting to. I wanted him and I couldn't believe he didn't know that. What he said in response surprised me. He had a relationship with another woman that he knew was not satisfactory. He had wanted to break it off before he had met me and it was gradually ending. He could not have two women at once. He needed to shed his Saturday night date before we could begin. Just as he promised me he did so the following week.

I could not ever violate such a man's trust. I knew he would not harm me. A man who cannot even date two ladies at once without suffering guilt, without feeling dishonorable, who must put it straight with the first before he can begin with the second, will not cheat, betray me behind my back. If this was the way he loved then I would love that way too.

There have been opportunities. I am at lunch with a man who has invited me out to discuss a book project he would like to work on with me. Before the coffee arrives he tells me he wants one more adventure in his life before age binds him to his home. I think he wants to climb a mountain or fly an airplane. It seems he wants to have an affair with me. He is appealing. He smiles at me. "What could be wrong?" he says. "It will be our secret." He offers a little excitement that won't hurt anybody. He takes my hand. I am pleased. When you are a married woman this does not happen very often. My feathers must still be shining. Why not? No one would have to know. I could play. I don't believe that sexual pleasure beyond the marital license is a serious sin. I don't believe in my immortal soul. My mortal soul gives me trouble enough. But then I think of something far worse than sin. I could hurt my husband whom I would never hurt, not for a second, and I would hurt him if for even one afternoon I went with this man and let him touch my body that knows so well my husband's body. I would defile the thing we do with each other in the bed when the children are sleeping. I am not sorry the man has asked me. A woman likes to know that her options are still there. But I am certain I will not accept. I am not afraid my husband will find out. I am afraid that my knowing will slide into my life with him, will destroy some absolute closeness we have achieved, will harm us both in some unknown way. I wonder if I am just conventional, afraid of life, too cautious for a swim in the wide sea. That is possible. But I have known what it is like to be alone in the world and I have known that I could not harm my love or even bring it into dangerous waters. Maybe this is fear. Maybe this is what we mean by love. I would not break his trust in me. After all my trust in him is the cornerstone of my life and all would tumble down without it. I drink my coffee and go home.

Monogamy has its price. But it has its rewards too. Would I be a more interesting person, a better lover to my spouse, a wiser woman had I met this one or that one in this place or that? I will never know. What I do know is that, reasonable or not, to be with another man in the ways I am with my husband is unthinkable, would violate the web of life we have spun together, would jar and tear at the very roots of our trust.

I know there are other ways of looking at this: other women play and consider it play. Other women do as they please, as suits them, other women are in marriages with men who disappoint in some profound ways and feel incomplete without the excitement and additional romance of an affair. I do understand that. There are men whose marriages have dried, who are contending with depressed or rage-filled wives, who are lonely beyond bearing. This is not a matter of sin, it is a matter of circumstance, need, soul. I myself can only be faithful, not because of a sacred vow, not because of the children (who are now grown and what I do is none of their business), but because I have something I do not want to bruise or crumple. I want my love just as it is for as long as fate allows it.

Does this make me a family values crusader in secular clothing? I don't think so. I don't believe that my way is the only way or the moral way to live. I respect the varied decisions people make about fidelity, the solutions they find to the stirring of their hearts and minds. I don't want to condemn anyone or legislate anything. What I do is my choice intended for my life alone. What others do is their own decision. We are all of us seeking to find safe havens, sparkling lights, warm spaces, to preserve the spirit. But how?

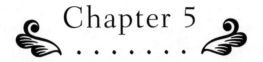

Chapter 5

When the Going Gets Really Tough, the Tough Have Children

Another burden that is also a blessing or a blessing that is also a burden is children. About every ten years or so some woman writes a book about how much better off women would be if they didn't have children. They talk about the financial and emotional resources that children consume. They talk about the imposition on a woman's creative energies and their time and how we are tricked by a society that does not have our personal best interests at heart into the act of reproduction. One of the arguments that appears in all these books is that children destroy love between the adults, they impose themselves and their emerging personalities into the twosome and soil the tapestry that the parents are weaving together.

These critics whose targets are both the bliss and the bane of most of our lives have a point. Children do put terrible pressures on a marriage. They reveal weak spots in as effective a way as blue light the police use to reveal blood spots. They change who we are, and what are our possibilities. Children affect where we can move and how much money we need and how free we are to change our places. Our well-being is no longer only ours. It includes theirs and so our happiness is held hostage to theirs which in due time may expose us to peril, potential misery, embarrassment, humiliation, and ordeals of suffering we might well have avoided if we had not fallen in step with the species and reproduced. It is perfectly clear to me that a marriage without children has many advantages over one with. I fully respect and understand anyone who makes this decision.

I have at certain hard points wondered if I had made a mistake in having children. If my work would have been more vital, if I could have made the language better do my bidding if writing were the sole subject of my life rather than one of the many competing demands on my time. Would I have been an American George Eliot if I had not been picking up my children each day at nursery school? Also I might have been a professional tennis player if I had continued taking lessons. It is true that I could have had an apartment in Paris, a safari in Kenya, a salmon-fishing trip to Siberia for a fraction of tuition paid. It is true that I might have had a dozen dashing romances each one of which would introduce me to new people, new geographies, new ideas. If instead of marriage I had chosen adventure what might I have seen and done, what wonderful material for books might have been mine.

Of course one never knows about the road not taken. But I know that if I were to choose again I would still be married and with children. This statement could be mere sour grapes. The pressure children put on marriage, the five thousand strains about what to do in this or that situation, the fear for them, the arguments between my mate and me about minor and major matters concerning the children, even our financial struggles, these have created the most vibrant colors in our marriage. Our love for each other is not a separate matter from our life as we lived it with our children. It is merged into it. Children do not so much distract or subtract from the love of one mate for another as intensify the connection, mold it in the shape of the family, give us a reason outside of our own skins to be in this world. Yes, on a given Saturday morning for a time we went to the zoo when we would have preferred the museum. Yes, on a summer's afternoon we went to the park when we might have preferred an air-conditioned movie. And yes, when things went wrong we had to learn not to retreat from each other. I didn't like his temper. He didn't like my anxiety. We managed and in that managing we added to our love. Our children gave us leaf-filled branches and roots growing down deeper into our lives. They did not come between us, they became a part of us.

Adam and Eve did quite nicely in the Garden without children and only began their family after the fall, which tells us either that Eden is no place for children or a place with children is no Eden. Taking one's place in the long line of history involves creating and caring for children who will be the future as their children will be their future. There is no rational reason that a person can't just drop out of this process and some do. But the pull on us seems strong. Darwin said it and it is so.

Our nature, planted deep in each cell of our bodies, drags us towards reproduction. Our relation to all living creatures creates in us a need to be parents that seems as strong as our sexual urges, as strong as our desire to live itself. To multiply and be fruitful seems not so much a promise made by Jehovah as an imperative driven by our genes, enforced by our culture. This desire to bear and nurture children seems to cross all boundaries, nations, races, religions, rich folk, poor folk and the rest of us in-between. In every corner of the globe, in igloos and jungle huts, in both climates harsh and climates sweet, reproduction is the point of life, at least until some divine revelation or appearance on earth ends the cycles we know and removes the passage of time and the inevitability of our personal death from our world.

As we have recently seen, many gay people of both genders when given an opportunity want to participate in the birthing and raising of children. Even in decades when giving birth so often resulted in the death of the mother, when the chances of surviving childbirth were worse than one in ten, men planted their seed and women brought to life baby after baby. When one reads the statistics of death in the maternity ward in Paris prior to the acceptance of Lister's view on the washing of hands, which at last brought an end to the deadly puerperal fever that was in epidemic numbers carrying new mothers off to early graves, one wonders how could any sane woman have let any man near her personal parts. Why didn't they all become nuns to save their lives?

Some animals give birth only in times when there is enough food for their young and when there is trouble such as flood or fire or large numbers of predators they may not give birth or not so often. Among people however this wisdom seems not to work. One wonders when looking at the faces of starving children in a famine-stricken area why the parents allowed themselves the possibility of birth for an infant they knew would likely die. Humans do, they just do, perhaps in part out of ignorance of how to prevent birth, perhaps out of habit, perhaps because sex is connected to birth and they are unwilling to give up the one pleasure that exists even when crops are failing and war is raging. But more likely the tide that pushes human reproduction has more strength than most men or women can resist.

Children are good reasons not to get divorced. But children are often part of the pressure on a marriage that causes divorce. We don't tell the children that because surely they are innocent victims caught in the marriage tangle of their parents but their very existence colors everything about a particular marriage, its optimism, its faith in itself, its courage to go on.

Barren

The potential for trouble begins even before birth. Everyone knows that difficulty conceiving is one of the great strains a marriage may endure. This is not simply because of the self-conscious routine that lovemaking may take when couples are attempting conception but also because of the great weight of the consequence of the pregnancy lost, the hope that was there, dashed. The daily living with wanting and not having takes its toll, the risk and expense and difficulty of the fertility treatments, the effort not to blame whichever of the partners is responsible for the difficulty is strong. The resentment of other couples who have easily borne children and the inability to express irrational or hateful feelings puts additional tension into the mix.

Many people go through long years of fertility dances and overcome the pressures this puts on their marriage whether the outcome is successful or unsuccessful. But infertility is hard on anyone's marriage, very hard. Not being able to conceive and bear to term a child makes a woman feel diminished in a very essential way. Not turning on her mate, not turning on herself, keeping the happiness of the marriage intact, this requires skill and gentleness and a good deal of empathy with the other partner. This is exactly as true for a man.

The biological part is not necessary for the act of parenting. But for some couples a failure to conceive can make a marriage tremble the way a house built on stilts behaves in a tropical storm. Since it is in fact the raising of the child that makes a parent a parent, where the real personal work lies, where the important messages of life are passed on generation to generation the adoption of a child will bring the couple back into balance, back to a place where they can do the thing that they desired. But the adoption process too is difficult and fraught with peril and disappointment and involves waiting and hoping and incredible strain.

Weathering the disappointment of the conception that does not occur month after month, weathering the disappointment of the call that hasn't come or brings bad news from the adoption agency, the lawyer, the doctor, the lab, requires enormous resilience and tests the depth of the partnership between man and woman. Because having children is so important to most people the lack of children becomes a reproach to the couple, a mutual failure they can hardly admit but one that haunts everything else in their lives sometimes leading them to leave each other.

When a couple has a child the marriage gains a new optimism, bounce, mutual interest and their investment in the future, in each other, in the community, in the world deepens. This optimism says, "What I am doing is good, who I am is good, my child is good, and things will be good for us, we are a strong unit, we are united, our bodies are good, our hearts are good, we will be good parents with amazing children who will grow up to be good if not exceptional people who will contribute to the world and be happy like us." This optimism (which always smacks of a raw naivete) is one of the better emotional states a person can fall into. It serves as a life raft for marriages through the exhausting years of caring for very young children.

The opposite of this optimism is the sadness of not having, bodies being wrong, things not going well for us, our unity threatened, our expenses high, our mutual commitment questioned. This is hard. It happens to many people. If all goes well this trouble unites instead of divides and deepens affection instead of shrinking it. The "if" in that sentence is a very real "if."

Some People
Really Don't Want Kids

Naturally there are people who resist having children: thank you very much, it is not for me. There are good reasons for this position. Sometimes this decision is made in the bleak light of an unhappy childhood colored by a political or personal trauma. These early experiences can leave in their wake such a dark view of existence that the adult may shy away from introducing a new being into the world. Sometimes the mental illness of a parent or a sibling seems like a danger to a potential child that shouldn't be courted. Sometimes a woman sees the unhappiness in her mother's life, a mother who devoted herself to her children who themselves could not respect her, a mother whose days seemed empty and who may have been depressed or drank too much or grew obese from the disappointments in her life. Seeing the destruction to their mothers' lives produced by having children some daughters vow never to make such a mistake. Sometimes a man had a father who deserted him or a mother who died early and simply doesn't want a child to suffer what he has suffered or doesn't feel he should be asked to give to a child what was never given to him. Some women and some men will tell you they just have other things they would rather do, become airline pilots, surgeons, truck drivers. They do not want to carry the heavy load of another person through their days. They want to live for themselves alone. They may be convinced they are protecting the environment and their childlessness is an altruistic act for the good of humanity.

Opting out of parenthood, or postponing it so long it becomes virtually impossible, if this is the mutual desire of both partners in a marriage, harms no one, certainly not the marriage. But what may nevertheless affect the quality of that marriage is the regret that can come later, the bad residue of each partner's past that lingers unresolved. A certain bitterness that curtails happiness may accompany this marriage or it may not. One partner may have rejected the idea of children with more enthusiasm than the other. This can become a nasty worm in the marital apple. I believe that intense if absurdly foolish optimism (a belief in the human project, with which one conceives and bears a child) is as good a tonic for what ails or will ail as any in the world and protects the marriage as it moves through the obstacles that lie ahead.

I have heard people say after the terrorist attack on the World Trade Center that they would not want to bring children into such a crazy world. This seems historically short-sighted. There were parents who conceived and gave birth while in hiding from the Nazis in World War II. There were parents who gave birth in the rubble of Stalingrad, or in flight from Soviet oppression, in the gulag itself, in DP camps, in the midst of civil wars, or while the British were burning Washington or the Goths were hammering at the walls of Rome or the crusaders were sacking Jerusalem. When the Chinese were suffering from famine and in the aftermath of great floods and hurricanes, some infant has always opened his or her eyes on the chaos around. The world has almost always been a terrible place where the fate of human beings is so often unfortunate that if we need to be certain that our offspring will have happy peaceful lives before conceiving them, we will have assured the end of the human generations.

Could the dinosaurs perhaps have become extinct not through meteors or climate change but because they lost heart and refused to conceive in such uncertain conditions?

The Dark Side

That is not to say that childbirth is a bed of roses or that all mothers greet their newborn infants with pure and unalloyed pleasure and joy. The ideal of mom, the flowers and the cards of thank you on Mother's Day are all very well, a means by which our commercial society can put a good face on family matters. But any sensible person knows that mothers can turn into witches and that life is no Hallmark greeting card. Maternal fury can rise at the demands of the suckling child. The newborn's crying and the neediness make some mothers feel helpless, insufficient, and rageful. Some women will turn that rage against themselves and become suicidal. Some turn the rage outwards and harm their children.

We know that a small percentage of women will sink into a biologically induced postpartum depression and some will be driven mad by the chemical imbalances in their brains and try to harm themselves or their children. The depression they are experiencing is part rage and part sadness. It can metamorphose into a deadly psychosis as the world has just seen in Andrea Yates who drowned her five children in the summer of 2001 in Kansas in the throes of just such a serious mental illness. She chased her seven-year-old through the house until she caught him and drowned him too. The scene is horrible beyond believing. She broke the trust we all have in the virtue of motherhood, in the protective instinct of mothers, in the myth of endless mother love, a mother standing between us and the cruelties of the world.

She became the wicked witch of fairy tale fame. We have always split our feelings about our mothers into two parts, the good mother and the wicked witch. We have always known, even if we have not put it to ourselves so clearly, that mothers do have hostile feelings and that sometimes they appear to us and to themselves as wicked beings ready to poison, boil, cook or drown us and unfortunately this plot line isn't restricted to fairy tales.

Andrea Yates's story was particularly dramatic but we continually have mothers who abandon their children to orphanages, hospitals, relatives. We have mothers who cannot mother and disappear on the first train out of town. We have mothers whose own needs are so great they cannot be giving and on duty twenty-four hours a day in the service of their offspring, mothers like Susan Smith who drowned her children in hopes of gaining the hand in marriage of an affluent boyfriend or mothers who allow their boyfriends to abuse their children even to the point of death, like Hedda Nusbaum, whose husband Joel Steinberg beat their little girl Liza in front of her unprotesting mother until the eight-year-old lay dead on the bathroom floor.

We have the story of Medea who betrayed by her husband Jason went into a rage and killed the children they had together. She was mad in both senses of the word and she is considered a rare monster, but what of the mothers, and there are legions, who use their children, harming them in the process, to torment the father who has divorced them or wishes to? What of the mothers who move far away from the fathers for no other reason than to punish the men they once loved by depriving them of an easy visit with their children?

Christians believe that God Himself sacrificed His only son for our sins. There are storied fathers who have sacrificed their children. Abraham was willing to do this for his God. Agamemnon did indeed kill his daughter Iphigenia in order to place the gods on his side of the war. The once-upon-a-time sacrifice of virgins deep in the continent of South America, the child soldiers offered to death by the armies of Africa are part of a human pattern in which the weaker and smaller become burnt offerings to some desired end. Adult men in positions of political power sacrifice their sons in wars and have always done so. Some Asian countries kill unwanted girl babies. All the talk about our human love of our children, our need to reproduce ourselves, takes place on a world stage where killing the children has always been a possible solution to the religious, political, demographic dilemma of the moment.

In fact all mothers feel rage at their children to some degree and at some time. The difference is that most mothers have so many good feelings that the negative ones which rise now and then pass on like summer storms and do not threaten the well-being of mother or child. To see a five-month-old baby smile as you enter the room, to see the small hands reach up for you, to run your hands over the smooth as yet untouched skin of a baby, to daydream about the future life of the child, to listen to the soft sounds of cooing, to watch the baby's eyes follow the up-and-down motion of a mobile, these things which seem so small and ordinary, so boring compared to the clash and bang of the world outside the nursery, can to each parent seem like heart-catching gifts, reasons to get up at three in the morning and reasons to give up resources, vacations, former pleasures, reasons so absolutely good that they are assumed rather than argued.

On the other hand profound exhaustion, sleeping only a few hours at a time makes anyone irritable, vulnerable to dark thoughts and afraid of what they have wrought. The way human biology works our infants are so helpless and dependent on the arms of the mother that resentment is just built into the package. Bliss it may be to hold a sleeping baby in your arms but it is not bliss to try to get a baby to sleep who is crying endlessly, seems not to be satisfied by any means at hand. Mothers who are not suffering from a clinical postpartum depression can still find this transition from a life for one's own sake, to a life lived in large part for another human being, often difficult and disillusioning.

There are homes in America where anger is considered forbidden and furthermore a sin. In such homes, and Andrea Yates may have lived in just such an environment, it is hard to find a release for the normal angers and disappointments involved in tending children. If you can't allow yourself a moment of hatred of the new baby or if you feel so guilty should one occur that you must run away from that feeling, push it out of sight, then perhaps anger becomes brittle, grows in strength, threatens a mother's life as well as the life of her child.

So even for women not suffering from postpartum depression, not clinically ill, there is an imperative to knit the anger at sleep deprivation, at endless demands on the self, into the pleasure and delight of the baby. By acknowledging the irritation, the inexorable imposition of the newcomer, the alarm that the new role of mother brings, into the daylight of acceptable thought, the hopefulness of the family endeavor may be preserved. Anger does not burn so dangerously if it is admitted to the party where it can take its place at the table among all the other emotions already there. There are so many things in America we find hard to talk about with each other, despite all the talk shows and confessional prattle that floats over the land. Temporary, passing anger at our babies is one of them and it is a dangerous omission.

But there are other angers beside the anger at the newborn that parents must deal with as time passes. The two-year-old refuses to come out of the bath. The four-year-old leaves building blocks strewn across the floor, the five-year-old whines and whines. The three-year-old won't eat what is on her plate. The seven-year-old won't come in from the yard. The ten-year-old won't do his homework. They all hit and bite and hurt one another. They push and take toys away and tease. The nasty human heart in the body of a child does not bother to conceal its desire to have, to take, to dominate, to eliminate rivals, etc. This can make a parent furious, sad, frustrated, and the wonderful optimism in which family life may have begun loses some of its shine or at least that shine on some days may hide behind dark clouds.

For me the fighting between my children which echoed the fighting between my parents created a noise in my head that would make me wild with fury. Even knowing that the world was not coming to an end because one was crying and the other was mean as she could be I would feel a despair rise in my breast that on subsiding would leave me weak, pale, profoundly shaken. The sound of cruelty, one child to another, is my weak spot, the place where I lose my sense of proportion. After all it's normal enough, this sibling push and pull, just close the door and ignore it, my mind would tell me while my hands would shake and if anyone had asked me at those moments I would have said, "Life isn't worth it, I want to escape now." Of course I wouldn't and I couldn't and I didn't really want to. But the moments would come and go leaving me with a recognition of my own unexpected flash-flood rage, the one that waited behind my eyes, not buried deep enough, in my psyche.

When a three-year-old runs off the curb and into the street a parent will feel a rush of great fear and when that three-year-old is safe again, pulled back onto the sidewalk, a parent will scream in fury at the child, will spank, will cry, will lose all control as anger mushrooms forth. There is real hate in this emotion. But this is a complicated hate. It has come because the parent loves the child so much and dreads so losing it that the threat of the oncoming speeding wheels has demolished the parent's control. Who has frightened the parent? Who is to blame for all these horrible feelings, but the child stepping out into the street? We become angry not for the first or last time at the being we love. It is the measure of our love that we have become so enraged.

This has everything to do with marriage. Because the children become a part of the marriage, the well-being of the children becomes essential to the happiness in the home and there is simply no such thing in the modern American marriage as a relationship between man and wife that is not impacted by, or kept entirely separate from, the existence and the experiences of the children they have brought into the world. Marriages may have been relatively untouched by children among those upper-class English people who kept their offspring in the nursery with hired nannies and then sent them off to boarding school. But in the modern American family the children are the fruit of the tree. If the fruit is blighted the tree may well wither.

Stormy Weather

How we endure the bad times in our children's lives, how we respond to our mates during these times becomes our history, much as the history of the Civil War is a piece of this nation's story, so how we managed our family when a child was very sick and needed a serious operation or another one was failing school or a third, in teen years, was withdrawing from our company and counsel is our history, our marital tome, the making of us as a unit. It could have been the unmaking of us as well.

One of our children at age twelve developed a bad flu which led to a pneumonia and days in the hospital attached to an oxygen mask. The initial pneumonia receded but many months afterwards she would still run fevers at the end of the day. Antibiotics worked while they were taken but when stopped the fevers and the coughing returned. She had developed as a result of the pneumonia bronchiectasis, which is a chronic inflammation of parts of the lung that antibiotics cannot entirely reach. They ultimately had to surgically remove a lobe of her lung and it was during the year of this illness that our marriage was most threatened. I could think of nothing else. I could talk about nothing else. I couldn't read or write or phone a friend. Until we found out that the damage to the lung was operable and that she could survive and return to health I was possessed, obsessed with her fevers, her sleep, her days, her doctor's appointments, her coughing, each cough ran through me like a needle. Of course I didn't want her to know how worried I was. Of course I couldn't hide it completely.

My mate on the other hand was a silent worrier. The more concerned he was the less he talked at all about anything. It seemed to me he wasn't there at all. He was quiet. He went about his work. I examined every detail of her day over and over. He seemed not to be listening. He responds to trouble like a wounded animal that goes off into the forest and lies beneath a fallen tree, hidden and alone. I respond by rushing frantically about looking for a hand to hold, looking to talk.

This difference in our personalities has many advantages as we aid and supplement each other most of the time but when this child was ill I felt alone with my terror and the aloneness made me angry at him. I thought he was angry at me. I thought his quiet manner and the walls he built around himself that grew higher and higher with each passing day were intentionally there to keep me out. When finally she was operated on and we stood together in the hall outside the operating room and I felt his shoulder against mine and his hand pressing hard in mine and I saw the grimness of his face as we waited and waited for word from the surgeon I knew that we were together in this whatever might be happening behind the closed doors.

When eventually they brought her down to the intensive care unit and there were tubes of flowing blood coming from her side and her small body was lying in a large bed intended for adult heart patients we both saw that her color was already better than it had been since she had first fallen ill. We were told by the surgeon and the pediatrician that all would be well and then I saw my husband bend and kiss her forehead with such gentleness that I was brought back to him with all the ripeness and full reach of first love.

There are different reasons why parents grow apart during a crisis with a child and if it is an illness that leads to death this will in our modern world, where the death of children is not commonplace, force each parent to see the other stripped of their normal role, without their usual protective garb. The sensitivity of both parents, the raw nerves that are exposed, can easily produce a conflict, a dislike of the other, a blaming or a withdrawing. The timing of these moods and high emotional feelings will never be the same in any two people. There are conflicts that arise as each may miss the increasingly acute needs of the other.

When a child is born damaged with a serious birth defect this puts enormous pressure on marriages. It breaks the shell of optimism that the partners held. Something terrible that no one expected has happened. If a child is born blind or deaf or with a hole in the heart or a disfigurement of face, or with limited intelligence, or suffering from any of the varieties of autism, the man and the woman may after a time of mourning the perfect child they had wanted go on to do everything in their power to give this child the best that the world of medicine, education, can offer. They can restore the wound to their pride by taking active roles in the world of research or care or fund-raising for whatever ails their child. They can partially restore their balance by going on to have other children who do not suffer from the inherited disease, the accidental mutation, the affliction of mind or body.

But there is no doubt that the disappointment is bitter, the pain of the thing as terrible as anything that can happen to the human being and the fallout of this pain is certainly pressure on the marriage as each couple loses faith in the goodness of their lives, in the future of their love and what it will bring them. There is a tendency to blame the other and the self even when obviously no one is to blame, as is most often the case. There is a tendency to turn on the self, if only I hadn't had those cups of coffee, if only I hadn't experimented in college with that drug, if only I had been a better person God would not have done this to me and the same is true of you whatever you did, whoever you really are. There is the wish to erase the entire marriage and begin again. This is very difficult for people to manage without hurting each other, without severing their loving connection. Even sex, which is how it all began, becomes now suspect, foe not friend.

We can see this clearly when a child is born with a crippling defect but the same mechanisms appear in other marriages when a child is simply disappointing in more familiar and less terrible ways. This one refuses to play catch with his father and prefers to listen to music with his mother. That one gains so much weight she is ungainly and seems to her pretty mother like an alien being. Children sometimes have a way of not being exactly what we intended, they are not our wishes made manifest. This too puts strain on our marriages. We give up our expectations very slowly and with great difficulty, each in our own way and in our own time. A father can turn away from the entire family in disappointment with his son or a mother whose daughter has just given up the piano lessons that were so important to her may arrange her work schedule so she is home later and later each night. In the process of learning who our children really are we may blame each other for what they are not, we may lose our joy in our family for a short time or a long time and with that lack of joy comes a diminishing pleasure in the marital bed or a diminishing desire to achieve in the world, or a general lowering of mood, a darkness in the house that affects all the members of the family and can end in estranging man from wife if they aren't very careful.

In every marriage there must be a time of disillusionment. The raising of children hastens this process. All of our weaknesses, all of our vulnerabilities, our childishness, our cowardliness, our courage, our differing styles of coping are revealed in the harsh light of time. I know a man and woman who had three children, two girls and a boy. The boy was a disappointment to the father who was an esteemed mathematics professor who had made some valuable contributions in his field. The boy was just not mathematically inclined. He was supremely uninterested in numbers. He was also uninterested in classical music, his father's other passion. He took piano lessons but refused to practice and exhibited so little talent that they were finally stopped. The child loved animals and stories and sports and was a great success on the playground. Still his father preferred to spend time with his daughters. One played chess with promise and the other seemed to have her father's mathematical gifts. The family went on a vacation in a trailer to tour the national parks. Someplace outside of the Grand Canyon they stopped at a gas station and got some soft drinks. They got back into the trailer, the children in the back, the parents up front, and drove about twenty miles when the mother realized that she hadn't heard her son's voice in a while. She called to him. She turned around. He wasn't there. He had been left behind at the gas station. The man turned the trailer around and they rushed back and found the child sitting at a picnic bench, his face stained with tears. But the mother thought the father had so little interest in his son that he had left him there, or hadn't thought to check for him, and this became the last straw in a marriage that was in trouble anyhow. Shortly after the family returned home the marriage ended. This was not the fault of the child but his existence affected the marriage in a less than helpful way.

Reading this you say what a terrible man, he should have loved his son no matter his potential, no matter his life's path. This is very easy to say about somebody else. We all have such precise and vivid pictures in our heads about our children and our relationship with them that we do get disappointed, are hurt, feel rejected, and in turn may reject a particular child. Sometimes the images we have of what our children should be get in the way of our closeness to them as they are. This is not sin. This is not the result of bad family values. It is just a banal human weakness that can potentially spoil any home.

We need to be proud of our children and proud of ourselves as parents. When a child stutters, or develops a school phobia or rashes no one can identify, or has severe learning disabilities or problems with aggression or wets the bed long after he or she should be in control, we as the parent feel responsible, and feel the child's flaws as flaws in our parenting. This too can excite trouble between mates. He wouldn't do that if you would only. He wouldn't do that if you would stop protecting, coddling, working so late, fighting with your mother, crying in front of him, pushing him to read, etc. And then behind that is the thing that none of us can quite put into words but if your child is not healthy of mind, shows a flaw that the other children in her class do not, there is the feeling that you, your spouse, your marriage are somehow to blame, caused it by some bad choice or series of bad choices or just by being not-quite-adequate people. This is a rotten feeling and can turn noxious in the context of a marriage. As "your fault, my fault, our fault" floats most often unsaid through the home it spoils the pleasure each member of the family takes in himself, herself. It is easy to understand how this mounting pressure can turn one or another or both parents away from each other and towards other people who are outside this problem.

Years ago while in college I visited for a month a commune in South Carolina in which a group of idealistic people lived together, farmed together and ran a toy factory. They were sweet, decent people, some very religious, some simply believing in communal life. I thought I had found the perfect place. The land was beautiful, the mountains beyond the valley guarded the commune like sentinels. The families, who shared a dining room and planned everything together, seemed so much happier, so much finer than anything I had ever known before. I did not have a mate and this was a community without single men, and reluctantly I returned to college to finish my education. I thought I would return when I was ready to have a family. Several months after I left, a man driving a truck backed out of his driveway and ran over his neighbor's three-year-old child who was playing in the gravel. The child was killed. This was an accident of course, but within another couple of months the commune had dissolved. Some of the members went to other communes and some returned to city life resuming professions or careers they had left behind. When I asked why the commune dissolved I was told the death of the child just did something to the air. No one wanted to stay there anymore. I think that the optimism, the faith that good works would bring good things, was broken and the confrontation with the random cruelty of the universe which the best communal living could not stave off punctured the hope of the enterprise, causing it to deflate like a balloon.

Problems with children serve a marriage like the death of that three-year-old. They threaten the union with more pain than it can tolerate, they leave hope shattered.

If the problems are emotional there is a certain shame and embarrassment even in our overtherapized, "let's talk about your phobia or your incest trauma" society. When my first daughter was three it was clear that she was fragile and excitable and while filled with talent and charm could hardly sit still a moment and anxiety drove her to a wildness that was hard for her, hard for me. She was always making scenes in public places and I was always feeling like a bad mother because I couldn't calm her. She didn't seem quite like other children and I could feel the disapproving self-satisfied sigh of other parents on the playground, at her nursery school, in the supermarket.

A divorced single parent, I knew what I had done. I knew it was my fault. I consulted with a well-known child psychiatrist. He explained to me that a third of the children like her improved over time, a third got worse, and a third stayed the same. As I left his office I tried not to let terror overwhelm me. I tried to focus on the third that improved: but improved how much? To stay the same was not good enough. To get worse was unthinkable. I stood on the street corner waiting for the light to change. It became green and still I couldn't step off the curb. I was suddenly afraid to move. A strange man asked me if I was all right. I was. I crossed the street. But that feeling of terror has never left me entirely and can be summoned up by the ring of the telephone, or a memory, or a voice even now. Before I remarried and she was adopted by my present husband and our family grew it was clear that she was a wounded bird, a child with inner storms that boiled up to dangerous intensity. My husband was strong and firm but often she made him angry. I was tender and frightened and pulled apart by her confusions and angry at him for being angry at her. He would yell. I would tremble. We argued over how much of our resources we could spend on her care, on her special schooling. I was impractical. He was practical. I wanted him to save her. He wanted me to keep perspective. There was a whole family to think of. Because she was trouble at school, trouble at camp, impulsive, explosive, suffering from terrible nightmares, I felt like a failure. It was hard not to let that failure or my guilt seep into the lives of the other children and keep my marriage free of the defeat that grew in my soul. To some extent I succeeded and to some extent I did not.

All around me now I see parents struggling with children with disappointments minor and major and I know that the original expectation that one's own child will be free of trouble, happy ever after is very often tempered as real life has its go at us. These are not children who have been unloved or unwanted. These are children from homes that did not intend to foster addictions, to sponsor dropouts, to lead children to cultish seclusions. It is simply that our personalities, lopsided, wounded in places, irregular, well intentioned or not, seem sometimes to produce children who are not as whole or healthy as we would like. We are not as whole and healthy as we would like. The genes we carry sometimes favor us and sometimes don't. This is as true of our mental life as it is of our physical life.

This doesn't mean that our children don't also succeed and surpass our best hopes. Many grow into fine adults with homes of their own and productive work of their own. Many troubles are overcome. But all is not perfect within the American family. If it were, no books, stories or films would be necessary. We could just rest content by the hearth and purr like a cat after his meal.

Parenting—An Equal Opportunity Employment

Marriages can go out of tilt if one or the other parent becomes more involved with the child than with his or her mate. A mother or a father can take second place to a wonderful child who is going to win the chess tournament, bring home blue ribbons from the horse show, excel in tennis matches, bring in prizes or simply seems more deserving of love than the other parent who has diminished in some way, worn thin in some way, seems less important than the hopes that can be found in the child. Parents may see a second chance for themselves in their children and then each success be it in baseball or academics becomes in some way their own redemption. If this feeling is intense enough it can exclude the other parent. Children do offer us a second chance to reach for the gold ring on the merry-go-round. This can enrich or distort a marriage. If a parent is forced out of the meaningful circle of a child's day he or she may drift off, turn away, attend to someone else outside of the home. Sometimes parents use their children to keep away, create distance from their partners.

How to discipline the children is a potential sore point between parents. We each have our own childhood memories good and bad. We want to do things the same way our parents did or in a completely opposite way. In some sense our children's childhood is a chance to show our parents how it should have been done. It is a chance to prove our wisdom and worthiness and we all begin thinking we will do better than was done before, we are after all by definition more modern. I had been cared for by nannies and wanted never to leave my children with a baby sitter. I wanted to care for them night and day so they would never be lonely for me. My spouse wanted the children to understand that we could leave but would always return. He thought that the better way to assure the children would not be lonely. He was right. I was wrong. It took us a while to work out this difference. I could almost never say no. He was always able to say no and loudly too. If our children were slightly confused by these mixed parental messages I can hardly blame them. Sometimes I was angry at my husband for his unyielding ways and he was surely angry at me for my acute desire to make everyone happy all the time. We each accommodated to the other in time. But I don't think he knew when he married me what a weak-spined lady he had gotten. I think I believed that because he was an expert in child psychiatry he knew everything and would never be angry or frustrated or overly firm. Ha on both of us!

What kept our marriage together through those early years? I trusted him. I admired him. I knew I could talk to him about everything I needed to, from the smallest to the largest of matters that weighed on my mind. I read Anthony Trollope novels because he prized them above all else. He read Virginia Woolf for me. We planned celebrations together, shopped together, we replaced carpets and curtains. I held his hand in movies. I let my shoulder brush against his as we walked down the street. He would not analyze my dreams but he listened to them. I could see his face when he talked in inaudible tones to his patients on the phone. I could see the sweetness in it, the worry in his eyes. When a critic attacked me he was grim. When I wrote well he was pleased. Our fortunes were permanently linked. I never doubted it. He never doubted it. Year by year, anniversary by anniversary, we built the home we lived in: our marriage.

Adolescence Terminable or Interminable

Because of our combined family my husband and I once figured that we were sentenced to about twenty years of living with teenagers.

There was the breaking of curfews. The waiting in the early hours of the morning for an errant child to return. My fear was that something had happened on a street corner, in a subway, somewhere my child was bleeding, hurt, and calling for me. Actually they were having a fine time likely doing something I would not want them to do. I was the one in need of comforting. When the door would finally open the mixture of fury and relief that flooded my body was powerful enough to cause a heart attack or so I thought. There were terrible long silences at the dinner table. There were whispered phone calls and pauses when I would walk through the room. My spouse was of a calmer disposition. "Leave them alone," he would say. "Let them figure it out for themselves." I was in a state of agitation. This one hardly ate anything. That one was miserable and haggard and not sleeping. A boyfriend disappeared and it seemed as if that daughter would never get out of bed and go to school again. There were nasty things said. They were critical or they were silent and their silence spoke volumes. One kept a diary she kept on her person in case I might be tempted to read it. This was probably wise.

Their rooms were cluttered with take-out cartons, unwashed laundry, sweaters in need of fresh air, papers, books, magazines, underwear, coffee cups, ash trays, bottles of wine stuffed under the bed. They lost all interest in the dog who now was walked by me. They lost all interest in everything in the house but the telephone. They lied about where they were going and with whom. My ability to protect them was shrinking by the day. Their need for me to protect them had almost vanished. It made me frantic.

I wanted to talk to them about sex and give them all my wise modern knowledge and I wanted to be sure they were protected against pregnancy. They didn't want to talk to me and cut any approaches short. I was lonely and feeling unloved. This meant that my spouse would have to love me more to fill in the gaps, to support the soggy soul. Moreover, because my children were now sexual animals I could look at them and see my own aging. I was not what I had been. This is natural enough but it made me sad, envious even of the fact that their time was coming and mine was nearly over, well not nearly over in years, but for catching eyes, for stirring interest, for sending out certain vibrations, yes, over. No wonder all this stewing around in his wife and daughters made my husband weary.

There is no doubt that our marriage suddenly seemed like a dry branch, no leaves to sprout forth, no grace in the household.

Across America as their children enter puberty parents tremble, marriages tremble and family confidence is battered and many marriages do not survive the storm. Was it always like this? Did fourteen-year-olds suffer from withdrawal, attraction to bad things, rebellion and peer pressure in Ancient Rome? Were the young apprentices in the guilds of Renaissance Florence threatening suicide, engaging in risky behaviors? Were the young homesteaders writing poetry by starlight about the loneliness of the human heart, starving themselves until they were mere bags of bones, or throwing up after dinner on the prairie grass? It's hard to know. What is clear is that in America today this period of time just before the doors to childhood slam shut is one of great and prolonged struggle for many of our children. This struggle has an enormous, occasionally mortal effect on our marriages.

The psychologists tell us that the teenager is fighting against an impulse to retreat into childhood, to merge back into mommy's arms, and an equally strong but contradictory desire for independence, adulthood, autonomy. One or the other of these directions might be easy enough to accomplish but trying to go both ways at once is enough to make a person go mad and some of those teen persons do exactly that. Maybe adolescence brings such a hard time in America because there is so long a wait between sexual maturity and the time when our culture allows the umbilical cord to be finally cut. If everyone got married at fourteen and went out into the world to form their own households these furious cooped-up beasts our children often become would be so engaged in surviving they would have less time for substance abuse or sexual experimentation and would just grow up, the same way they learned to talk and walk: easily.

But in the world we live in we need our children educated. We need them to sit still and listen like little children long after the time when their bodies are well prepared for action. We also want them to be individual people, not cookie-cutter molds of their parents or their friends. We need them to think for themselves, to feel for themselves because that is our definition of the free citizen we want them to become. On the other hand the choices we lay before them can be overwhelming, so many things they can do or be. Soon they will be able to live in any part of the country they choose. They will pick their own mates. They will make their own way.

We raise them as if they are never going to be pushed out of the nest and on their own and then we push them out as if they were seven-day-old sparrows. Naturally they protest. Naturally they feel lost. Hormones raging, always homesick for a home they know they must leave, they drive around in cars going no place. They party and grope each other as if the answer lay in the peer group, each member of which shares the same fright and the same desire for life ahead. Living with a teenager is like living with a Mack truck in your parlor, wheels churning and churning, but all that happens is that your carpet is chewed up and the noise is unbearable.

All the fragilities of their earlier lives have caused cracks that now turn into chasms in their beings. I have taught writing to adolescents and I dread the not infrequent story in which the main character commits suicide. As a teacher I don't know if the story is a cry for help or a cliché. I will attempt to find out and the squirming writer will likely not tell me the truth one way or the other so I'll have to guess in a situation where anyone's guess is as good as mine. The image of an inner earthquake, an inner ice storm, an inner eclipse of the sun, all these can portray the adolescent soul at one time or another. Parents experience guilt as this child or that one shows signs of trouble and then blame each other, blame themselves.

We read of Columbine with incredulity. How could the parents not have known there was an arsenal in a son's bedroom? We read of the instances of teenagers shooting schoolmates with a small element of condescension or contempt. Why didn't someone see it coming? What's wrong with those parents, divorced were they? When we hear of a teenager found hanging in his garage or dead of an overdose in a back alley we get the same tightness in the stomach and then we have the same defensive reaction: what was wrong with those parents, was it a working mother? Was it an alcohol-abusing father? And with these thoughts we banish the evil eye from our own homes. However, the fact is that mental imbalance, including psychotic hallucinations, are not as uncommon as all that in our teenage population. Every emotion is stretched to its limit, the good and bad ones alike. Feelings of separation, isolation can easily get out of control. Rage at others, rage at the self can, like the pumping bass that carries the song along, push actions later regretted. The fact is that unhappiness, terrible psychological distress, leading a child to want to destroy himself, leading a child to cut herself, pull out strands of her own hair till there are bald spots for all to see, leading a child to put needles in his or her arm, or swallow pills that will derange the mind, grow like weeds in our garden and are so common that no one should be surprised at the most extreme eruptions. Severe emotional pain exists in tight religious communities and in suburban streets, it exists among teenagers in private schools and boarding schools. It is hard to understand why we are so blighted but blighted we are. And with every one of those troubled children comes parents in trouble too, marriages placed under pressure, homes that once had expectations getting used to reduced expectations.

There are a burgeoning number of wilderness schools that attempt to provide discipline for the over-the-edge teenager. Junior boot camps they are with rigid rules and demands and they do seem to hold some kids back from falling off the face of the world. But the parent who drives his child into the cactus hills of some distant state is feeling like a failure and feeling like an outcast himself. No parent says to himself, "Well this just happens in America today." Instead they think I have failed my child, maybe I yelled too much at my wife, maybe I shouldn't have been divorced, maybe I wasn't home enough, maybe I'm like my own father, cold hearted or selfish. Marriages rock and collapse under these thoughts. The self-doubt, the fear for the child, the thought that there is something rotten in the foundations of the house that has caused the child to fall apart is so disturbing that some parents flee the home, or themselves turn to excessive drink or food, or retreat into religion or work. We don't have enough psychologists to help all these people with this burden. We don't have the financial resources to support the parents who need support. We can't even support those children who show obvious signs of out-of-control anger, not to mention those who will never harm anyone except themselves.

At Columbine the parents seemed unaware of the taunts of their children's classmates. It doesn't do any good to reproach parents for not knowing what is going on with their children. The doors are closed to their rooms. The children are not talking to them. They are nodding yes and slinking off. Their real lives are with each other and their parents have become like shadows on the wall, spooky but not real. The best behaved of teenagers is carrying around enough secrets for a lifetime in his or her backpack. In their new loneliness these parents will either turn towards each other or away. How the marriage fares depends on this choice.

The high-school world with its rankings and conformity and nasty underground rumor mills is as tough a place to survive as any. There is something shocking in the word "freaks." Many of us whose households lacked teenagers at the time of Columbine had not previously heard the expression. A freak is an outcast. A freak is something ugly, distorted, scary, the antithesis of harmony and grace. A freak belongs in the side show, extra parts, missing parts and all. And some kids think of themselves as freaks and other kids are rejecting and cruel to those so labeled. What are they? Too fat, too shy, too awkward with the opposite sex, too vulnerable, too unathletic, too tall, too nervous? If I were the parent of a freak I would be beside myself with concern. I would run not walk to the nearest psychotherapist. I would question my marriage, my husband, my self. What had we done wrong? What caused this terrible bump in the road? What were the earlier signs? I would feel my child's exclusion as if it were my own. For this reason among others they might not let me know. I might be the last to know. There is nothing harder on a marriage than the failure of a child to succeed at any phase of life.

This means that in order to survive the turmoil in their older children the married couple needs to trust each other, to let the other one take over when exhausted. It means pretending you are not in a state of despair when you are so you can go on. It means learning to live with a certain knot of fear in the belly. It means that man and woman need to cleave to each other and find the things that are meaningful in their lives in the arms, in the talk, in the work of each other. We say at the altar "for better or for worse." But we never imagine how bad the worse can be.

Yes, some adolescents are good to the core and behave well, lovingly to parents, sweetly to younger siblings, never stay out late, show no symptoms of anxiety and aside from listening to loud music are the very model of model citizens. Some children just sail through what upsets others. Maybe good parents get good teenagers, at least that is what we would like to believe. Maybe troubled parents who are themselves living on edges get troubled teenagers who are withdrawn or violent or take knives and make little cuts on their arms and legs, but I'm positive the correlation is not so neat. The epidemic of teenage pain we have in this country is affected by something beyond the way we parent, by the very difficulty of growing up as our culture expects us to do.

My daughter with the diary was graduating from high school. She wouldn't let me help her buy a dress. She didn't tell me she was getting a prize. She did allow her parents and siblings to go with her for a celebratory dinner at a Chinese restaurant that evening. She did not look at me through dinner. She accepted our congratulations without a smile. To love and not be loved back, to be excluded from your child's pleasure and triumph, is hard, very hard. As we sat at the table and the meal was cleared away and the younger ones wanted to go off to their own party my eyes suddenly filled with tears. A milestone had been celebrated but the celebration was hollow, ironic, unworthy of the name. I felt my husband's hand on my leg. I felt him stroking my leg, the way one might soothe a cat who's been frightened by the sound of thunder and whose hair is standing up in shock. I felt the warmth of his hand on me. Had he not touched me in the right way and at the moment I needed it would we have fallen away from each other? I doubt it—by then there was too much history, too much trust for one moment to sever our mating. But it was good he was there. I needed him.

Only in the rankest of sentimental made-for-TV movies do children bring joy to a marriage. What they do is drag the adults into the thick of the forest where adventures lie, where demons lurk, where wildflowers bloom around moss-covered rocks, where mettle is tested and courage is needed and life is lived to its fullest. If the task does not drive the couple apart it forges a permanent link between them. It is our child whose drawing we are staring at in the first parents' meeting of the prekindergarten class. *This child* is the one among all the others whose splotches of red and blue rivet our attention. *This child* is imbued with a fascination, an importance, an aura of life like no other simply because it is ours. This intensity of glance at "ours" follows through celebrations of birthdays, graduations, weddings, and attaches itself to the grandchildren with almost the same ferocious power to absorb, to underline time, to give meaning. This is, perhaps, a folie à deux that can unite a marriage, becomes the loom on which the marriage weaves its story.

But if someone is counting on children to bring them peace of mind, self-confidence or a steady sense of happiness they are in for a bad shock. What children do is complicate, implicate, give plot lines to the story, color to the picture, darken everything, bring fear as never before, suggest the holy, explain the ferocity of the human mind, undo or redo some of the past while casting shadows into the future. There is no boredom with children in the home. The risks are high. The voltage crackling. I would not confuse this with joy. But it is as far from the silence of the grave as one can go.

Chapter 6

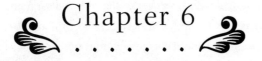

Triangulation, Strangulation, Genograms

The psychologists have given us a phrase that has been picked up across the country. We now know that there are "dysfunctional families." I hate that word, *dysfunctional*. It makes it sound as if some of us are machines whose cogs need oiling, whose thermometers need adjusting. It makes it sound as if we are all meant to behave in one way and then some of us fail. It is a word without charity, mercy or reality and behind its technical sound there is a negative judgment forming. With some dreadful deed someone has been bad. Using this label is a way of holding your nose while sticking it into the deep personal pain of disappointed, frustrated, saddened people who are living together in sorrowful ways. It is a sophisticated way of name calling.

Family therapists have observed this weird tendency in marriage to pull in a third party and work out problems between the couple on the head of the extra wheel. They call this *triangulation*. It is perhaps the source of the mother-in-law joke. What appears to be happening is that the couple unable to deal with his anger at her or her disappointment in him turns on the mother-in-law of one of them and she poor creature, maybe innocent, maybe not, becomes the focus of their mutual anger. In this they glue themselves together and the fight becomes with someone outside the partnership, and the fight then does not threaten the couple one with another. The trouble with this maneuver is not only that it makes the mother-in-law unhappy but that it usually doesn't serve the purpose for which it was designed. Sooner or later it breaks down and whatever was bothering the couple in the first place raises its ugly head once more. There is just so long you can rail against members of your spouse's family or your own. Eventually it becomes like a broken record, the energy in the fight goes away and there you are still angry about something.

Some people use the boss for this distraction. The young couple can focus on the injustice in the office, the vulgarity of the person in charge, his or her blindness to the gifts of the worker, etc., and ignore the fact that she is aching for more sex and he is unable to give it or he is wanting to be hugged at night and she unable to sleep in a bed with him has moved into another room. The young couple can hide their disappointments and disillusionments with one another by focusing on the terrible crimes of her faculty adviser, his ex-girlfriend who calls from time to time or any other convenient person who unbeknownst to themselves can play a part in a play they may not even attend.

Some couples in which one or both partners had a bad childhood with memories of insult still burning can focus on their childhoods and send their hateful feelings backward in time to parents, their own, their partner's. This too serves as a fireworks display that can disguise the problem closer at hand.

As long as it isn't covering up something rotten between the couple this kind of distraction is as harmless as the allergic sneeze. But sometimes it allows the couple to stay in a deep rut, to have the same conversations over and over without any movement toward easing the tension, towards understanding each other. Life offers so many convenient possibilities for this kind of triangle trouble.

As a species we do love leaving someone out. Folk wisdom tells us that if three people set out to sea in a very small boat only two of them will return. Among any three high-school girls who are all friends two of them are talking about the third in less than complimentary ways. The secret alliance between a man and his lover against his wife may be part of the delicious satisfaction of the affair. A woman may whisper into her new partner's ears all sorts of treacherous comments about her spouse that deepen one connection but weaken another. We can see that this is a game that people play but it is a very sad game indeed because at the end all of the participants are apt to be calling "Olli, Olli, all in free" long after the dark has fallen and the home base has disappeared.

We begin perhaps as Freud has said in triangles, mommy, daddy and baby. Baby may grow into a three-year-old who wants mommy all for himself or a girl who wants daddy without mommy attached. Here is the Oedipus on which we all hang our first loves and that follows us ever after. In adult life we may re-create those days of envy and wish and frustration for ourselves. We may be excessively jealous or excessively fearful of loss or we may simply have given too much of our vital energy to mommy or daddy and as a result our adult lovers receive only a drastically reduced portion.

Family therapists draw genograms that describe the problems in families back a generation or perhaps two. They can show people how some of their fights echo and simulate those of their parents and even their grandparents. They can show with their graphic designs how failures of parents to meet the needs of their partners get reenacted with the new couple, distrust is passed on, fear of abandonment is passed on, alcohol abuse, child abuse is passed on, failure at jobs is passed on, the battle of sibling rivalry can be decided on the basis of old stories—this one looks like Uncle Joe and so I love him more as I loved Uncle Joe, that one has my mother's dimple: may both child and mother rot in hell. There is no doubt that the past is never dead and buried but continues to thrive in our souls as we, not deliberately but with brilliant unconscious attention, replicate the troubles that surrounded our childhoods. People do have an uncanny ability to do this.

A father leaves his children to go to another country and seek a better job and the left-behind family spends ten years reading his letters, waiting for him to send for them, and then once arrived in the new country, now an adult, married himself, one of those children may take a job that keeps him far away from his own home for long periods of time. A woman whose father ran off with a lady friend leaving her mother to fend for herself and her three children may fall in love with a man other than her husband when her child is exactly the same age as she was when her father abandoned the family and she too may move away, leaving her child behind. There is uncanny truth in these diagrams but not all the truth there is, not the whole story.

Family therapists tell us that one member of a family may be unconsciously chosen to suffer a problem such as a school phobia, bed wetting, or more seriously, anorexia or delinquency. The child may be showing these symptoms in order to keep the family from noticing that the parents have lost connection, are angry with each other. The disturbance in the family may not be exclusively within the child who seems so troubled. When the relationship of the parents is altered and the depression of one clears up or the anger of the other fades the child will be freed of the symptom and released to his or her own life path. This kind of tangle of man and wife and child is hard to unravel but it can be done.

The thing that rouses suspicion about this formula is that since the family therapists believe this pattern to exist in most cases, they seem always to find just what they are looking for. If they were looking for something else it's likely they would find that too. Yes, trouble occurs in a social context and trouble in a marriage will produce an anxious child who may indeed create a diversion from the marriage with a noticeable cry for help. But is that all that is going on? Is the child a mere paper cutout attached by the hand to older family members or is there something awry in the child's own mind that is running wild with fear, with anger, with despair?

We are far closer to understanding each other than we were at the start of the last century. We know there are forces at play that exist just below our awareness. We know that we are subject to influence from our childhoods, our earliest loves. This is good. We know that every identification is not a gift and if you are identifying with a miserable mother or a drunken father you can be in bad trouble. But if we feel that we have solved the mystery of family life we have been fooled.

We are no closer to mass happiness than we ever were. We just talk about it a lot more.

Human beings are simply too complex, too unpredictable, too filled with potential for growth and change and sudden veering to the right and left to be simply creatures of their family history. For the most part we would have a hard time laying a graph of any kind over our spirits, our memories, our actions. We glide, we slide, we twist and turn with our difficulties. We just don't stand still like dead butterflies pinned against a board. We are harder to understand than that. We are predetermined in many of our choices and actions but we also have free will and the potential for wisdom and insight and change. It is important to understand, to see, the patterns that might sandbag us into horrible repetitions of the least desired parts of our childhoods and good therapists help us do just that. But have no doubt we are not machines. Although subject to the laws of nature our souls look more like a Pollock painting than the Ten Commandments embroidered on a pillow and set out in the parlor on a chair.

We are affected by our temperaments which are perhaps genetic at base but also influenced by the earliest of touches, the oldest of events. We are affected in whom we become by our imperfections, early illnesses, the death of a parent, the closing of the town mill, the war that took a parent away and returned him paralyzed. We are formed in part by our siblings and our attempts to both compete with them and distinguish ourselves from them. If an older brother loves music we are apt to take up skiing. If a sister is shy we may develop majestic social skills. Who we are is crisscrossed with the times we live in: how many druggies panhandling on the streets of Haight Ashbury would have been cheerleaders if they had only been born a decade earlier?

When we enter into marriages we bring our past, yes, but how, in what way, what language can we use that can truly capture our experience, our selves?

In-Laws, Siblings and Other Minor Characters That Appear About the Hearth

Can you fail at being an in-law? Of course you can. Is there a formula, a manual that comes with the role? Of course there isn't. If pop culture is right one of the big problems in marriage is the meddling in-law, the domineering mother, the pathetic or hostile mother, the parents who burst in at all the wrong times with the worst advice in the world or an overwhelming need to themselves be the center of attention. If we were to assume that life is really reflected in laugh lines we would listen to all those mother-in-law jokes and assume that a marriage to an orphan would be a blessing indeed. But in the real world too many mothers of married men and women live far away across whole continents. In the real world of today I think the parents of a married couple are almost like birds that have done their job and when the chicks fly off they resume their own flight without a backward look. Our nuclear families on the whole seem to need more not less family to help and support them. But the exact and proper relationship between the generations has not been declared or defined in any clear way, leaving us to understand our roles through sitcoms, through repetitions of, or reactions against, the way our own parents behaved towards us.

We are all muddling about. I admit that as a step grand-mother I am not the baby sitter that my stepdaughter had hoped for. I have too much to do in the world myself or so it seems from my point of view. I can be counted on for emer-gencies but not for the day-to-day needs a working mother requires. For that she had to hire someone. In another era I might have been eager to be the chosen baby sitter. In another era I might have wanted to tell her that I disapproved of this or that in the choices she makes but as it is I admire her juggling of things, assume that my way of setting a bedtime is not the only way and hope that I am still a meaningful person in her life. Am I? Maybe, maybe not. Does she want me closer or fur-ther away? Where is the line on which I am supposed to stand and never cross and never stray from? The question makes me nervous.

My husband's mother had died long before I met him and his father shortly after we were married. My mother died before my second marriage and my father was an absentee parent and grandparent. No fuel for comedy there. But now that I am someone's mother-in-law I can see that the role is delicate and it is very easy to take a misstep, a fatal misstep. There is a comment in Genesis in the verse on the creation of Eve:

> *"This one at last is bone of my bones and flesh of my flesh. This one shall be called woman, for from man she was taken." Hence a man will leave his father and mother and cling to his wife so that they become one flesh.*

This is a beautiful image but it doesn't explain about in-laws since Adam and Eve had none. It leaves the parent who spent so many years nursing and tending, worrying and paying for, working for and dreaming about his or her child suddenly abruptly outside the intimate circle. The parents of grown children have always known this would happen, the transition from the baby who cried when they left the room to the adolescent who can't wait for the parent to leave the room has already occurred and yet there is a sense of violation, of being cut off that can occur as the young married couple makes their own circle and invites only their own children into it.

The verse in Genesis telling man and woman to cleave to each other would never have been written if there wasn't some tendency on the part of adult children to hold on to their parents for dear life making their spouses stand to one side while the parent-child drama continues for better or worse until death do them part. Going home to mother after a fight is not cleaving. Telling your mother all your grievances about your spouse is not cleaving. Taking money from your parents and not telling your spouse is not cleaving. Those lines in Genesis would never have been written if all parents could easily give their children in marriage without tugging at them ever after, without requiring a rekindling of the home fires now and then.

I seem to have contradicted myself. But we've all seen the results in real lives of both kinds of in-laws. Yes, in America parents of young couples are often not available for the support that is needed. It wouldn't take a whole village to raise a child if grandparents were on the job. And at the same time some other parents have trouble letting go, staying out of the way, serving as stewardesses rather than pilots on their children's flight to wherever: "Coffee, tea, or milk?" is really all that is required of them.

I know that when a husband sides with his mother against the wife on the smallest of matters, the correct use of a fish fork, the price of a pair of shoes, this can make his wife roar with pain. I also know that a mother of a daughter can love the man that her child has brought home to be her spouse and then feel brokenhearted when the marriage breaks up and the man disappears and never speaks to her his formerly beloved mother-in-law again and what had seemed like a real family connection is exposed as a cheap yard sale item, tossed out with the wedding pictures.

Our emotional lives are passed on somewhat like our genes, jumbled, merged with other lives, but present somewhere in the mix that becomes our offspring. If that is so a mother-in-law or father-in-law will see the past repeated in their children's lives and their own mistakes writ large. Yes, every one is free to mold themselves and is responsible to themselves alone for their souls but at the same time parents are influences, shadows, voices in the dark that whisper helpful or unhelpful things even when they are silent or dead or live in another country. Parents may simply have to watch in horror as marital accidents (our own faults tossed back in our faces) occur. Alas.

I have a friend who has told me of a forty years' hate on her very long-lived mother-in-law who made her feel uncomfortable at the table, inadequate as a mother and wife. My friend's husband never tried to stop his mother's harsh criticisms but he never stopped his wife from complaining bitterly to her friends about her mother-in-law either. Sometimes a spouse can express anger at a parent that the parent's own child could not or would not and this is good for the marriage, allowing the wife to mark the distance from the mother that the son desires but needs help in achieving. On the other hand that unwelcoming mother-in-law spent over forty years without the affection and respect of her daughter-in-law and the daughter-in-law spent the same time insulted and offended, without the second refuge the mother-in-law's home might have provided in hard times. The sad part of our bad relations with our own parents or our spouse's parents is that we lose the possibility of sanctuary that might have been provided. We go two by two, cleaving yes, but exposed to all the bad weather without so much as a raincoat a mother-in-law or father-in-law might have provided.

When my children were young I would sometimes take a walk on the most expensive street in town and stopping in children's stores purchase fancy clothes that we could not afford and did not need. I bought the clothes that I knew my mother would have bought for my children, would have expected them to wear, if she had been alive. At that moment I was neither cleaving to our budget nor my husband. There are times when cleaving is just too hard and the dangerous riptide of the past too strong.

Once my remarried father who wintered in Florida came to our house in New York City to celebrate his seventieth birthday. We had not seen him for over a year. Our phone conversations were stiff and dull. The history between us was hardly smooth. But for this occasion I had invited my brother and his wife and child, my own stepdaughter, and my father's stepchildren, three boys and a girl who were all young adults. His second wife was supposed to come too. On the day of the party she called and said she had stomach trouble and could not fly up from Florida. We assembled, my younger children passing crackers and cheese, the older ones decorating the room with flowers and balloons. We had champagne. My children and her children had nothing to say to each other since we lived in different universes, had different educations and ambitions. Some of the children made faint attempts at general conversation, others lapsed into heavy silence. We had made a beautiful poached salmon and we had a cake with candles. My little girls and I had made cookies that had the word "Grandpa" written in white icing. As I looked out over the awkward dinner table I realized that we were not a family and all my best china (given to me by my mother) could not make us one. I did not make a toast to my father. It was my first seventieth birthday party and I didn't know that was customary. He was angry that I did not make the celebratory toast. As he was dying some years later he complained to me again that I had not even made a toast that evening. I should have. Was it mere ignorance that stopped me? I have never since that night, except at my father's funeral, been in a room with his second wife's children or his second wife. Whose fault?

Now he was married and was right to hold to his wife's family above the family of his first wife, above his own children. I think. On the other hand I was right to try to bring us together and make us of a larger family that could serve as root and shade tree all at once. His present wife was right to avoid the birthday dinner and all visits to our home because that way she remained uninvolved with his children or grandchildren and it was therefore easier for her to become his sole heir and receive all his money for her children. I was naive to think it might have been otherwise.

In the real world, family, in-laws, married couple, divorced couple work out an elaborate dance, each watching out for itself, each jockeying for some kind of advantage, a gain in money or in love, power or protection.

I want my daughters to marry but I recognize that if they do I won't be able to talk to them so often, so intimately, so urgently. I must move back and let them cleave to their spouses and leave me perhaps to play again as I did in early childhood with imaginary friends. I will do this graciously I hope.

This cleaving business is perhaps harder than it seems. In times of illness, financial stress, a rock slide on the marriage road a son or daughter may turn back to his or her parents for comfort, for assistance, for support that for one reason or another is now sparse in their own homes. How much comfort is the right amount? How much support is a loving act and how much is tug to return to the original hearth and who ever knows when a little love turns into too much? We are all in the dark, children and parents. In this individualistic culture we put so much emphasis on successfully separating from our parents (just listen to kindergarten teachers' demands on five-year-olds) that we forget that we need our closed circles, our family, uncles and aunts, mothers-in-law and fathers-in-law. And independence is a lovely thing for a nation but not a value that trumps all others in human affairs.

When the family values folk are trumpeting their vision of the virtuous life what they mean is that girls should not have sex before marriage and abortion should be unthinkable and that divorce is not something good people do and that stability depends on everyone obeying the strictest of social rules. But there are other ways to interpret the idea of family values. I would think that absolute loyalty to one's children and their children is a family value. I would think that love of one's sister's or brother's child is a family value. I would think that offering one's mind and soul to your in-laws, older generation to younger and younger to older, would be a family value.

This often involves money. How alone is each generation in their economic struggle? This is a question decided now family by family. Wealthier families tend to have patriarchs and matriarchs who set up the younger generations sometimes debilitating them in the process. Poorer families tend to split off and spin in their own directions. Honor thy father and mother is harder to do without financial ties and in their place financial responsibilities. It is part of the failure of family life that so many old people are abandoned and lonely and that so many young people are without families to love or parents to lean against.

So while we see marriage as a discrete entity, a happening of sorts up on a stage of its own, we forget that marriage lives and breathes in a social context, in a family that existed before and will exist after the marriage of the particular couple. In India the custom of the bride making her home in the groom's family house makes this explicit. It seems to an American eye like a dreadful idea. It makes the young bride the servant of the mother-in-law. It means the son does not cleave to his wife but obeys the rules and the desires of his mother. It means that it takes years of life for a man to become head of his own house and for a woman to live without another looking over her shoulder at all she does. The horrible tales of brides burned because dowries were deemed inadequate or because they were disliked by mothers-in-law or sisters-in-law are proof of the insanity and inherent cruelty of this system. For us the loss of independence and autonomy for a married couple would be unthinkable but perhaps we overvalue independence and make a fetish out of autonomy. That's why we live in a society with so many lonely people drifting at our edges. Are we really in the long run better off than if we adopted the Indian style of family life?

Sisters can be so close that one feels left out or isolated by the closeness of the bride to her husband. Brothers can be jealous of the mate of the other, they can feel irritated that the couple now does things that do not include them. A wife can look down on a brother-in-law or the brother-in-law can look down on the wife. The web of dislikes can grow dense with plot complications and ultimately catch the married couple in its sticky threads. My sister-in-law found me less than lovely for reasons of her own. My stepdaughter found my brother impossible and would say things that would leave him bitter and furious with me. My father's sister was not welcome in my childhood home because my mother found her vulgar. My aunt would not have dinner at our house because she found my father rude. My uncle thought my brother was arrogant and my brother thought my uncle was limited in mental capacity.

All these opinions and tugs and pulls weigh on our hearts and while they do not make or break a marriage bond they become part of the weight that is carried, part of the daily rough tramp through multiple relationships. At the very least they can create fights between a couple. Cleaving to each other or not a lot of other people hang around and can behave very unpleasantly. So it is.

The bands of revelers that in some villages follow a bridal couple to their bed and make noise all night may never disband. You can't choose your mate because you think his or her relatives will be easy to deal with. You take your chances and assume that you'll just have to get used to that banging at the window for the rest of your life.

Too much aloneness American style is hard on a marriage that has to carry all the emotional baggage on its slim shoulders. Too much togetherness brings a cacophony of problematic relationships into the house. The right balance, the right way to live in a family seems to have eluded us. We're stuck in a minefield and trouble waits no matter what direction we move in.

Chapter 7

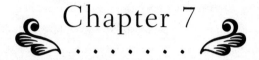

Talk, Talk, Talk

And should everything be put into words? This question is answered by a resounding affirmative by the therapeutic culture we live in. Men, who tend to reticence, are being asked by their wives, their therapists to say aloud what they feel, what they think, what they know. Women, who fall more naturally into the swim of introspection and communication, are spending more and more energy examining themselves and their partners. Across the land there is the drumbeat of therapeutic lists being made, investigations into the marriages of grandparents. The men are from Mars and women from Venus themes have caught fire and while another generation might have accepted differences in male and female response this generation wants to erase them, examine them, and reach out across them. Which in principle is fine but seems to result in a cacophony of words many of which are mouthings, repetitions, going around in circles, and sometimes harmful. The author

John Updike said, "Most marriages are ruined by too much communication."

What he means is that honesty is a virtue but not always: that telling your partner everything you think or have done or want to do is not always helpful. Words out of the mouth can't be taken back. Descriptions of old lovers, or new dalliances, complaints about mothers-in-law, angry remarks that belittle or humiliate, reflections on other people's virtuous behavior intended as invidious comparisons can deal a marriage a mortal blow. A constant focus on what you did and what I meant and how you made me feel (all of which are good in the right dose) can become lethal if overused, or used without mercy, tact, or understanding of how they will be heard. "I've never been attracted to women with big hips," is not necessary if your wife has just gained a few pounds. "When you talk baby talk when we make love it makes me want to throw up" is not the right way to put that thought. "My first boyfriend always gave me my favorite flower on the anniversary of the day we met" can only create trouble. In our therapeutic, *let's talk about it* culture we may talk our marriages into the ground. There is something to be said for discretion, for biting the tongue, for holding back. Communication is fine until it isn't.

If a marital infidelity has occurred is it the right thing to do to tell the spouse? If the affair was a casual event, in another city, meaningless in every way, is it necessary to tell? If the affair is more serious and ongoing then what? But if the betraying partner is not sure what he or she wants to do about it, then when and what should be said? Can you really ruin the intimacy of your marriage by omission? Can you ruin it by revelation and in the name of honesty bring down the roof over your head and the heads of those you love? There is no one answer to this question. Since both options are true. Sometimes in some circumstances it is better not to tell everything. In some other circumstances you must tell because the bond between the married couple is stressed beyond bearing by this silence. Sometimes it is better to wait a while and hold your tongue. The individual story, the nature of the players, the plot of what is going to happen unfolds as a result of this decision. But we are a country so in love with the idea of ourselves as honest and forthcoming and ready to tell all to the camera that we forget that some secrets should be secrets after all. No you shouldn't keep from a child the story of his adoption and no you shouldn't hide the fact of Aunt Minnie's mental break-down but maybe if it will cause more pain than can be borne you can keep to yourself the not-so-happy story of the two-night stand you had with the man you met at the gym. Maybe you want to use the transgression to get out of the marriage. Maybe you want to use the transgression to make your partner improve, reenergize, court you again. But maybe not. It is in the texture of the particular marriage that each such decision needs to be made, never by an outsider, never on a general principle, never out of a misguided sense of virtue one way or another, and never never never by a therapist.

I would want to know. I think I would want to know. Am I sure? Not exactly. Would I tell? Maybe, maybe not. If it was important, yes. But if it were casual, naughty, bad behavior because I was angry about something, or feeling old, or anxious in a strange place, I don't know. I really don't know.

We may have confused the therapy room with the marriage bed. We have confused the TV talk show with life itself. In therapy everything on the mind needs to be said. In therapy there is no discretion, delicacy allowed and the therapist is trained to accept all our thoughts as grist for the mill. A spouse has a very different mill. And life stuck as a guest on an eternal afternoon talk show is surely a form of purgatory that one wouldn't wish on one's worst enemy.

My first husband told me that when it came to women he preferred straight-haired blondes. I am not. He told me he preferred women who looked like Lauren Bacall. I do not. He was being honest. He was being cruel. But his telling me or not telling me really didn't make any difference in our marriage. What was wrong between us was my misplaced affection, built out of my own peculiar needs and his own dark demons that would have made it impossible at that time for him to love even a woman with the straightest blondest hair in the world. There was no way that we could have communicated better and in so doing heal our differences.

The problem lay not in what we said but in who we were. And who I was I needed to explain to myself. He had no desire or interest in hearing it. And the more I understood him, the clearer that became. Words, despite the fact that he was a writer and I would become one, were irrelevant. My understanding of just where I was as I lived that marriage came through the daily experiences of our lives. I saw the way he ignored the child. I knew he was driven to leave the house at dark and return at dawn. I knew that he needed fame the way a vampire needs human blood and that he might die without it. I knew that he knew more about logical positivism and modern philosophy than anyone I had ever met and yet I could see that he was miserable, eaten up from the inside, and despite my regrettable illusions on the subject it came clear that philosophy and wisdom were not identical, and happiness was a third matter that seemed to have no relation to intellect. Words did not bring me to this insight. Certainly not words we shared between us.

It is peculiarly American to think that everything can be fixed if we can just find the right things to say to each other.

My husband and I enjoy (enjoy may or may not be the right word) a running fight with each other that has been going on since we first met. It goes like this:

Me: Slow down—you're up to eighty.

He: I am not.

Me: I can see it on the speedometer.

(He slows down.)

He: I'm not at eighty.

Me: You were.

He: I'm the driver here.

Me: There's no need to pass that car.

He: The guy's creeping. You want to be here all day?

(Switches lanes.)

Me: Be careful.

He: No, I'm driving with my eyes closed.

Me: There are cops out here.

He: You're on their side.

Me: For god's sake stop passing everyone.

He: I'm not.

Me: You're tailgating. We're not in a hurry.

He: He doesn't belong in the fast lane.

Me: That's the fifth lane we've been in the last five seconds.

He: Look you want to drive, you drive.

Me: I'll just close my eyes.

He: Good idea.

(*Fight over for a while.*)

We don't fight very often. This is our big one. And it's an important one. He thinks he's a World War I flying ace or an RAF fighter pilot. He thinks the road should be his, tra la, tra la, like Toad of Toad Hall. He thinks he's leading the pack and dust trails in his wake and the sky's the limit and the purr of the motor is the om of the universe. I think we live in a dangerous world where at any time I expect to hear the crunch of metal against metal and see blood, mine, his, spilling across the highway. I want to go home. I want both legs on terra firma. I suspect other drivers of irrational or murderous thoughts. I have no wish to hurtle through space. I don't understand that desire. I think it's going to get me killed.

Many things are at stake in this argument which is why it has lasted through so many years. His sense of himself as king of the road, as a man riding out on his cattle ranch to teach those rustlers a lesson, "just who is top gun around here," requires a certain speed on the highway, a kind of maneuvering around the slower cars, a dash between the lanes. My sense of myself as nurturer, woman as civilizing restraint, as alarm system for the family at large, requires me to say, slow down. We are stuck in our roles. The family therapists would say that he expresses my desire for speed, adventure, freedom and I express his bottom-line desire to live until tomorrow, his realistic survival sense. He can count on me to restrain him and I can count on him to thrill me. If we became one person we might have one sane drive through the perils of life.

Once in the car we can act out our old-fashioned, imprinted-in-a-prefeminist-childhood maleness and femaleness and while I get frightened again and again he gets angry at me, "All right you drive," he yells like a record stuck in a groove. The fight I suppose allows him to act like the beast in the jungle and me to play my part and somewhere we must like this game or we would have stopped it long ago.

But the game is much more complicated than it seems. He is a man who began his professional medical life wanting to save premature babies. He is a bread baker and knows how to make a child stop crying and he is the restraining arm against my quickness to judgment, my more mercurial emotions, my unsteady and sometimes feckless impulses. So if you read our marriage as pathetically gender stereotyped from our argument in the car you would misread us. If you thought we were using our car rides to reassure ourselves that our sexuality is in place according to the divisions learned in childhood but mostly abandoned in adult life you would still not have it right. If you thought that this is a power struggle about who will dominate whom—I am the bossy female trying to tie apron strings on the free-wheeling male, he is the male oppressor, with his foot on the accelerator able to bring fear into his wife's heart with the slightest pressure downwards—you would be seeing us through a social lens not from the heart of our marriage where he is my protector and I am the keeper of the key to his soul. If he tries to dominate me I am like a breeze that can't be commanded. If I try to dominate him he becomes a volcano hard on the outside, fiery within. You would be wrong if you thought you could understand our marriage as a power struggle pure and simple.

If on the other hand you suggested we should go wherever we're going by train, you would be completely right.

There is such history in a long marriage, so many minor crashes, a few major ones. We understand each other so well and real life seems not to stand still for theories turning them all into partial truths, sometimes truths, distortions if taken too seriously. Some fights are just the music of the relationship reaching crescendos, turning tail on itself. Only fiction could do justice to the way we ride in our car, only through fiction could a trace of our real voices be found.

There is in marriage a mysterious center, a core of whirling emotions, a very private and strange kind of poem that rises in the days and nights that pass. Marriage cannot be successfully subjected to analytic probing, to therapeutic insight. It remains mysterious, illuminated only by its own light, and not an object that can be bought or dissected or stolen. It can reek of evil. It can be sweet and gentle, it is always personal to two people. It is both holy and profane and there is no "how-to" book that comes close, comes near to penetrating the mystery. The great novels tell us how much there is to understand and how little we will ever understand.

In Sickness and Health

It's only gossip but reliable gossip. I heard that a well-known law professor had left his wife because she was diagnosed with multiple sclerosis. I was told that he had said, "I don't want to live my life with a sick person." It's very rare that someone would come right out and say a shocking thing like that. But it may not be so rare that someone might think or act with such gall or appalling self-centeredness. But I do know of several men who were not able to resume their sex lives with their wives after mastectomies. I know of several divorces that followed on the diagnosis of breast cancer.

On the other hand I know of a man who was ready to divorce his wife who had refused to allow him into her bed for many years and between whom nothing remained but the ash of their first love but when his wife became ill with a life-threatening blood disease he canceled his plans and remained in the house. What frees one man may bind another.

We make the vow for better or worse, we promise to be there in times of sickness, but these words are all too easy to say when nothing has gone wrong and very difficult under pressure of actual illness, when the mate can no longer do his or her part, when the illness itself has stolen the mate's vitality, beauty, interest in the world, capacity to hope. We know what we should do, all except perhaps that law professor.

We have the powerful and moving report of John Bayley on Iris Murdoch's long bout with Alzheimer's in his book *Elegy for Iris*. He took perfect care of her. He watched over her as her wonderful mind emptied out and she was reduced to an anxious obsessive child who understood nothing and could contribute to his happiness only by her silence or her sleep. He tended her body and steadied her mood at home until a few days before her death. The portrait he gives us is one of endless sacrifice and love which by the very nature of her illness had to be unrequited. But in the details he chose to tell he reveals his anger at her. He describes her loss of bladder control. He describes her messes with food. He lets us see her as she would never have wanted to be seen. This is his anger expressed in the guise of truth telling, reporting from the battlefront of a horrible but all too common human experience.

Theirs was a complicated marriage as are most. She was famous as a writer. He was only another Don among others. She may have preferred women. She certainly had relationships of long duration and fierce intensity outside of their marriage. He may have loved her but he may have been bound to her in ways that contained fury as well as love. All our marriages contain hostility as well as love. Then when she became ill he behaved with incredible gentleness, tenderness and honor towards her. But before she was in her grave he told all to the world. I'm glad he did and believe that the book is a document of importance to us all. But I recognize that he was angry, angrier than perhaps he knew. The harsh demands of anyone's illness are not suffered without reaction, without the selfish voice within pounding on the soul, making demands and cursing when those demands are unmet. Who in fact soothed, tended, loved John Bailey through those difficult years? That was the cry right there under the text. The thought that must have sustained him through those days was his determination to write it all, to reveal it all. There would his anger find its outlet. He is only human.

I'm not talking about the down days brought about by minor illnesses such as the flu or a bad back that strike all of us at one time or another. It is easy enough to bring a cup of tea or a couple of aspirin to the bedside but very hard to make visit after visit to the mental hospital where your spouse is being treated for suicide attempts, unlifting depression, manic episodes, psychotic thoughts.

When unions were sacred to God and no divorce was possible people endured the long and crippling illnesses of their mates as they had no choice. They may have found other loves on the side but they did not as they could not desert the ill spouse. But in this modern world loyalty is a choice and honor is a choice and self-sacrifice is not necessarily demanded by a modern world that also respects self-interest, supports an individual's right to be happy, and sanctions our desire to drink our lives down to the last drop.

Therefore if a man or a woman stays beside a mate who has been struck down, paralyzed in an accident, suffering from a long and debilitating illness, they do so because the alternative is not a personal option, because their love is so strong they could not imagine doing otherwise, or their sense of duty, obligation, sense of right and wrong ties them to the bedside. There is something beautiful in this. There is something holy in this. It brings tears to our eyes. But at the same time there can be something ugly in this sacrifice, something unexpected may grow in the space between man and woman and the disappointment they both experience. Self-sacrifice although it is applauded in saints does not always serve to make us better people. Sometimes we just become grim, bitter, dried up, or enjoy too much the dependence of the other, or enjoy too much our own discomfort. From the outside such a home can seem proper and just but from the inside the very same home may have monsters in the closets, termites in the beams and worms among the bed sheets.

A famous writer I knew had a stroke in his later years and became particularly dependent on his wife whom he had betrayed often in his younger years with student after student. When he was without strength she mocked him, she talked of his imminent death to his face. She bossed him around. She made fun of his limitations. She did not protect his pride. This was ugly to watch but on the other hand it was justified revenge for other times when the power balance (his fame) had been tipped in his favor. Sickness brings an opportunity for old scores to get settled. Sickness is planted in a familiar soil. Just as there are no hibiscus in Alaska so there may be no mercy in a marriage.

When the veteran returns home in a wheelchair we applaud his young wife who stands beside him. When the policeman with a spinal cord injury attached to tubes from all his orifices and breathing with an oxygen mask over his face is wheeled before the cameras by his loyal wife we ache for them both but we feel that all is right in our moral universe. Then we forget about them as they go on day after day and the young wife cannot have a second child and she cannot go on a vacation to Disney World and she cannot go out to her sister's wedding and she has no man to put his arms around her in the middle of the night when she wakes with a nightmare and she has no man to go to the PTA meeting with her and she sits beside his hospital bed now moved into their wheelchair access–ready house loving him less than she feels she should and suffering from guilt in addition to deprivation. We only see the heroic picture in the newspaper. We don't see the daily wear of his so compromised life. If we did we might not be so pleased she is by his side.

A tragedy that hits a man will usually run over his wife as well. A disaster that befalls a wife will fall on her spouse at the same moment. Love and honor will bind the healthy to the sick but rage and bitterness will join the enterprise. The sick will resent the well. The well will try not to but will be angry with the sick. The sick will feel guilty at harming the life of the well and the well will feel guilty for every fleeting second of resentment, of restlessness, of impatience with the sick. This guilt will make it hard to take the needed time away from the bedside. This guilt will provoke us into harming ourselves in a myriad of small and large ways. This guilt will be hard to shake and may stay with us ever afterwards. The misfortune of one will poison the happiness of the other. The binding together of two lives makes for double the risk of disaster. This is part of the marriage gamble. If we were a species gifted with the power to see into the future there would be many more people left at the altar.

Serious sickness brings with it a power shift. The once important CEO requires that someone change his sheets. The unimportant housewife whom no one wanted to sit next to at a dinner party is suddenly the executive with all the cards in her hand. Sometimes helplessness is itself a kind of power. It can provoke guilt. "Where have you been all afternoon?" In many ways the sick one can control the well one. In many ways the well one can betray the sick one.

We are all afraid of being sick and in pain, of being unable to do for ourselves and left alone in the dark of the night. We are all afraid of unmerciful ends. As well we should be. Our families are scattered and our children do not have the same obligations towards us as they may have at earlier times. They are unlikely to take us in when we come knocking on their doors. We certainly can't depend on our neighbors as was perhaps possible in other times. They probably don't know our names and would not notice if our mail was piled up on our doorstep for months on end. We can absolutely depend on the fact that our government will be as cheap with us as possible, as ungiving as permissible by law. We are clear that the state, while it may not let us starve, has no obligation to see that we are allowed to keep whatever dignity might remain our portion.

So while it is unromantic of me to say so there is no doubt that marriage is a kind of insurance against disaster, a way of taking a gamble (odds influenced by gender and age differential) on having a caretaker at the end of life, or an advocate in times of illness. All those older men tilt those odds in their favor when they manage to marry much younger women. They do so for the obvious reasons but as a side benefit they receive a private nurse for their last years. I do not judge this harshly. Every animal does what it can to protect its own hide and the human animal who will use his position or his money to win himself a bride in whose face he sees a potential nurse is behaving with legitimate self-interest providing he hasn't bumped off or deserted a previous wife in the process.

It is fear of the future illness that makes our birthdays, our anniversaries, our celebrations of graduations or weddings so poignant, so brave, so defiant of fate and so important to us as signs of our survival, our determination, our good luck. Marriages have plots, stories of their own. There is no story without threat, complication, obstacle. Marriage is a tale in which ever after is not a possibility.

Sickness takes the measure of a marriage. But once again what that measure is and what that marriage can stand and cannot is so personal, so related to the tales of the partners, to their own pasts, to the guilt that they bear or cannot bear, to the self-destructiveness or self-assertiveness that plays on their acts that we cannot from the outside always tell who is behaving well and who is not. We don't always know what is best for the sick partner or the well one. There are few rules that make sense in every situation. Some people are too eager for self-sacrifice. Some are not eager enough.

How Hard Times Can Bury a Marriage

A person can lose a job or make a catastrophic investment that threatens the well-being of the family and when this happens, and it does happen in every country every day to more human souls than filled all of Dante's Hell, it is Hell. When we think of marriage we like to believe, each of us, that we of course will go on loving through the bad times as well as the good. We like to think of ourselves as becoming stronger and finer under fire. A confrontation with reality, a quick turn of economic events against us, and we find we are not so noble, not so strong as we had imagined. As our marriages stagger from the low blow of fate or fault we may find we can be petty, carping, cringing, come down with headaches, drinking problems, leave dishes in the sink, snarl and snipe at our mates just as if Hansel and Gretel lost in the woods instead of holding hands and proceeding onward had bickered over the turn of the road and each gone on alone.

It's not supposed to be this way but it is. Nothing takes the shine off a man more than economic trouble. Nothing makes a woman seem less desirable than a sudden failure at work. In some way we need our partners to be successful not only for real reasons such as bills, tuition, debt to be paid, but for the aura, the glow, the optimism that comes with doing well.

My first husband was a playwright. We were very young when his first play opened off Broadway to rave reviews. We celebrated that night until dawn. As the bars closed and the sky above the near-empty streets grew ghostly pale and the neon signs reflected down on the glass windows we rode a flood tide of joy. I thought things would never be hard again. I planned to quit my job as a receptionist and have a child. We careened through the streets of Manhattan triumphant as ancient conquerors of great cities. The sweetness of the thing was mingled in my mind with intense love for him and vindication for me. This was proof of my good judgment in selecting what seemed like an impoverished and debauched young man from the very far side of the tracks for my mate.

But then came the next play which opened on Broadway two years later. By then I had understood that his success had not settled his spirit or given him strength and it had not made him able to stay at home without his hands shaking, his legs trembling, his drinking increasing until he would pass out. By then he was tempted by the world of glamorous writers, producers, famous people who wanted to have dinner with him, a drink with him in bars. He had no need of my company and I was lonely and left with a child. His fame was ash in my mouth.

The play that opened on Broadway was panned, not a little but a lot, made fun of, ridiculed cruelly. On opening night we read the reviews at a party at a beautiful restaurant with blue lights blinking in the palm fronds. He left the party alone and went drinking for days and days without calling or letting me know that he was alive and well. I went home to our baby. By then I knew we weren't in this together and not forever. I didn't stop loving him then. It took a long time and many aftershocks for that affection to wither and change and eventually die down to indifference or something close to that.

The fact that a terrible reversal of fortunes drove us apart was important. If we could not hold on to each other in hard times what were we together for? If his pain was his alone and not to be shared with me, how could I share his triumph? Had the earlier scene been a fake, an illusion? Now he might have gone on to write other better-received plays. He could have endured the pain of the bad notices and proceeded but for him the blow was mutilating, destroying and he didn't have the buoyancy to survive it. If he had turned to me for comfort or sustenance we might be together still but he turned away. Bad times are good indicators of the state of a marriage. Three months later he left the apartment with a suitcase. We did not part because of the play's failure. We parted because the failure of the play exposed the fact that there was no "we," that I couldn't save him from himself and should stop trying. He left me because I was no longer a talisman of good luck. Our mutual endeavor had crashed. He left me the way one leaves the scene of an accident, quickly.

There are men who are so ashamed of a failure that they can't face their families and they run away. I suspect that during the depression the railroads carried many such men in different directions all away from the persons who loved them. But if a marriage can contain the disappointment of one partner or the other, can struggle through economic reverses, or professional failures, if a man and a woman hold tight to each other when the world seems most rejecting, then marriage serves its purpose. But if bad times sap all the energy, bring out the worst, kill the hope that originally kindled the love, then marriage, always a fragile matter, can be damaged beyond repair. It's all very easy to say the words, "for better or worse," but to mean it is another matter entirely. We are selfish creatures after all. To stay with a man who has lost his ability to support the family, to respect him and never resent him, to keep on acting cheerful against the evidence, to fan the flame of erotic love under those circumstances, that requires a heroic effort beyond many mere mortals. These are thoughts I file under the category of money, money matters. Not just money but good fortune matters. What happens to a marriage is not always ours to shape. Fate, luck, history, the outside universe, they get to play with us and our marriages. No avoiding that.

Take One Step Closer and I'll Scream—Take One Step Back and I'll Scream

No one wants to be swallowed up by their beloved. "I love you so much I could eat you up" is something Grandma might say to her grandson who hopefully isn't listening too carefully. But if you read the popular literature about the inadequacies of men you see again and again that they seem to be in retreat. Silence is what they may offer in place of conversation, listening, or physically moving near. And of course it's not just men who pedal backwards from a mate. Women too have a way of removing themselves when the emotions seem too intense. The right distance from someone else is something we intuitively know when we are standing at a cocktail party. We don't get right up into someone else's face. If we do the other person will automatically back up. But what exactly is the right distance from someone you love and need? If that person backs up it can cause a panic in the heart and a rush forward which may only occasion more backing up. Closeness is desired by partners in marriage but *closeness* is a word that represents an ideal and reveals nothing about amount, place, and how to achieve it. One person's closeness is another's nightmare of suffocation. What seems like a comfortable distance to one person appears to another as if he or she has been dropped into the Sahara without so much as a camel or a compass and asked to find the way home.

This all stems from the first hours of our babyhood when things weren't as simple as they looked. We wanted to hold on to our mothers without whom we would surely die. Babies understand the life-and-death importance of this matter before half a year of life has passed. As infants we would like to merge into our mothers' bodies and in so doing possess them without risk, without parting ever after. At the same time there is a great push in the human soul for independence, for standing up on one's own two feet and walking about wherever one will, unattached. What joy we see in the face of the toddler who gets to his feet and moves forward and away from his pursuing mother. So before our first year is out we are caught in a primary, very perplexing dilemma: we want to be close and protected and a part of our mothers and at the very same time we want to be free of them, on our own, a contradiction, a seesaw problem, a difficulty that will follow us all our lives and certainly into our marriages where all over again we can dramatize the issue. I need my space. I need you. Where will it end?

Sometimes in the divorce courts that's for sure. When you ask a man what he is thinking you very often get the answer, "nothing." It is not that he is thinking "nothing," which is probably impossible to do without a frontal lobotomy. It is that he is quiet and removed and thinking his own private thoughts and likes it that way. Sometimes a woman finds this alarming. He is not there for me, she thinks. He doesn't love me, she thinks. He has erased me, she thinks as she looks into his absent eyes which are not focusing on her, not at all. She may demand his attention. Cry, bring up a subject he has to fight with her about like his mother's request that they visit her in Florida or whatever other unpleasant matter is near at hand. Like a plant in need of water if he doesn't respond to her soon she may begin to shrivel, shrink, go dry.

The word the professionals use is *autonomy*. He needs his autonomy or so he thinks. She needs her autonomy and so she can't lay her body down next to his whenever he wants her to. This can turn into a power struggle. This seems like a problem that a little patience and good will could settle. But unfortunately in the daily warp and woof of needs this tug can explode and cause a marriage to fall apart. He needs to play golf on Saturday and she needs him to be with her all day. She is lonely for his company. He has had enough of her for a while. Switch the genders around, the problem remains the same. The woman can be the one who needs the distance and the man the one who is always trying to burrow closer. She may feel comfortable at a certain distance from him and he may feel comfortable with a completely different placement of their souls.

Further complicating the matter is the fact that as very small children we all get angry at the mother we need so desperately. When at about a year of age we really understand that mother is a separate person and that we cannot survive without her care we feel angry at our helplessness and angry at her.

You can see this in the way a baby will suddenly pinch or bite its caretaker. You can see this as the child enters the terrible twos screaming when thwarted in the simplest of matters. We are angry at mother for frightening us with her comings and goings, for our inability to control her whereabouts. This anger mingles with our attachment to her and drives our need for independence. In marriage these feelings are replayed but now are disguised with adult concerns. We become angry at our spouses at the slightest sign of separation. Each partner wants to be the one in control. When we merge too far into the other or we lose a battle of control (a simple thing, what movie shall we see, what friends should we have, where should we go for vacation), the implications may make us feel furious, rotten, as if we were infants caught in that old old struggle.

Love is supposed to cover over these differences and it may for a while. Love makes one partner try very hard to please the other, to allow the other into his space or to trust the other if they are further away than would be desired. But love also makes us demand to be loved, makes us especially frightened if we think we are not loved. Loving someone does not make us content—it drives us on to be loved back. "I don't want to get devoured but I do want to be near or near enough." We easily become angry at the person we love. No wonder marriages reel around like drunken sailors in a bar.

And how we handle this matter depends on what has happened to us earlier in our lives. Has a parent deserted us leaving us afraid of connection or trust? Has a parent tried to control our every action and make us into an extension of themselves? Have we been loved for ourselves sufficiently or are we like sieves always thirsting for reassurance? What frightens us, what soothes us? The little quirks and habits of our personalities come into play. How jealous are we of others? How fearful of betrayal? How much aloneness do we need, how much can we tolerate without becoming a wreck or wrecking our homes?

Psychologists tell us to teach our children to sleep in their own beds. In our world where the individual is prized for his own accomplishments keeping an infant bound to one's body for too long a period is considered a disservice, leaving the child unprepared for the aloneness that modern life requires. On the other hand a child uncomforted, a child unattached becomes less than a child, less than a person. So a balance has to be maintained. This is true of lovers, i.e., marital partners also.

When we were first married I waited on the stairs of our house listening for the sound of the door to my husband's office to open, signaling the end of his work day and his return to the home. I waited patiently, sometimes with a child on my lap, sometimes alone, running back and forth making sure all was well with the children. For several years this waiting came with a peculiar lump in the throat, a speeded-up heartbeat and a tremor in my fingers. I knew he would come, but what if he didn't? What if some unpredictable thing had occurred, a patient had killed him, a blood vessel had burst in his brain, a robber had entered and left him bleeding on the floor? What if he were not to come? I sat on the stairs and ached with love and anticipation of loss.

After enough time had passed I no longer sat on the stairs at the end of the day. I assumed he would open his door and return. After enough time had passed we could be in a room together without conversation, without physical touch, each absorbed in some thought of our own, and I would not feel lonely. We had found our balance. This was love without devouring, without chasing, without terror, at least most of the time.

Sometimes I think I was made to be a native on some South Sea island who was never expected to be without companionship, body warmth, communal activities. I am not so impressed with the goal of autonomy. It seems to be one of those ideas sold to us along with the virtues of capitalism and exercise that are disguised as virtues to cover up their bitter taste. But I have learned my mate needs his space, his dignity, his distance at least part of the time. When we have trouble in our family he is silent and builds a wall around him that I cannot climb. When he has even so small a disturbance as a bad head cold he doesn't want me hovering about. He prefers like a sick dog to be off by himself in a forest of his own invention.

The difference in men and women on this matter may or may not be as consistent as pop wisdom would have it. But it is hard to tell how much of this *distance required* and *distance despised* gender style is a part of our culture (the way boys and girls are raised even in these more enlightened times) and how much is built into the anatomy and hormonal biology of the sexes. Perhaps men are hardwired to report that they are thinking about "nothing," when asked, and perhaps women are hardwired to bridge the silences with conversation, as intimate as possible. But perhaps after a thousand years of female equality we will no longer see one sex or the other so frequently following the maps laid out by the ancient and outdated stereotypes.

All that we know for sure is that on top of themes of domination and submission marriage is also telling a story that has to do with nearness and closeness. We are a veritable symphony of discordant themes. No wonder it is so hard to make harmonious music together.

Bad Men—Wicked Women

When you listen to a bunch of helping professionals talk and talk some more you get the impression that marriages fail because of miscommunication, because of the bruises that the past has made on the souls of the participants, and that with proper understanding and changes in techniques of relating one to another almost any marriage like a sailboat tipping on its side can be righted and made to sail forth again. It is true that, with the exception of the few Rosemary's babies that may be out there, all of us are products of our home life, as well as the vulnerabilities of our genetics and the errors therein. However we could say that about Hitler too, which illustrates well the fact that evil may have arrived at the table with an excuse but at a certain point the excuse doesn't matter. All that mental health chatter can cover up a basic truth: some people are bad. Some people can't be saved by therapy, medication, or thick applications of hope. And the people who are married to those folk are in deep trouble and if anyone can help them, the help must be to offer a way out.

Here is an alcoholic who hits his wife when drunk and beats his kids and some talk-show host is sure to suggest a good rehab place to turn things around. But everyone can't be turned around and some people simply do not have the capacity to empathize, to love another human being, and their rage is so strong that whatever you do for them they will again and again harm the more vulnerable around them.

We see men who cannot tolerate closeness to a woman and must run away from the twoness of a marriage over and over. They are emotional deserters forever in flight. They do not love, they conquer, and they must do so over and over again and therapy, time or age may not change a single thing in their behavior or mend their crooked hearts.

We have paranoid personalities who suspect their mates of betrayal and that suspicion will poison every dinner, every evening of that marriage till all remnants of love have fled and no therapy will penetrate the stubborn dark fortress out of which the paranoid peers. These are the jealous men who cannot let their wives out of their sight. Who are prone to beat them and hound them and consider them possessions without human needs of their own.

We have men who are so passive they cannot hold jobs or initiate a trip to the movies. They do not play with the children or take the car for new brakes. They seem like zombies, people in whom the light has gone out. Medication may help them, it may not. Sometimes they are so depressed that they are on the edge of killing themselves. Sometimes they do kill themselves. Rarely they take their families with them.

We have men who prey on their children and lose control sexually and abuse their own offspring. They may have their reasons but we know that they are bad men, men who do great harm and whose sickness is never acceptable and like a deep tumor in the brain, hard to remove. There are not as many of these men as the emerging feminist culture would have had us believe and they are far more prevalent in novels of recent decades than they are in our actual homes. Nevertheless they are there and they do evil, are evil and their unholy acts cannot be easily prevented—no hygienic spray will save us from men who commit incest on their children.

It's not just men who are bad. We have women who cannot control addictions to drugs or alcohol. They may refuse help. They may deny the problem. They may retreat from their mates and their children and finally abandon them altogether. We have women who cannot control their rages and hit and burn and harm their children. There are more of them out there than have been counted or reported in our cultural wars. But everyone knows a story or two. There are psychotic women who see the devil in their own child and try to beat him into submission. There are women who cannot get out of bed and work in the home or the office because of depressions so deep they are beyond the reach of doctors or hospitals.

There are women who are mean, just mean to their spouses, to their children, women who create homes in which everyone is afraid and uncomfortable. Their meanness may take the form of picking on a child or attacking a husband night after night or screaming at or accusing a mate of financial dereliction, sexual failure. There are people who cannot control their own meanness so angry are they. A friend's mother told her she would not buy her a bike when she was eight years old because she did not deserve a bike. This same mother would not attend her daughter's high-school graduation. She told her daughter that she was not pretty and no man would have her. How can a mother not love her daughter? It happens. What kind of a soul is that? What could that marriage have been like? What terrible things did she say to her husband after the daughter went to bed? There are women who will make a man feel weak or incapable and then enjoy his discomfort. We've seen women do this in public to their mates. There are men and women who are simply cold fish. They cannot truly feel affection for another human being. They may seduce others in a constant chase for a feeling of connection that never comes. They may appear handsome or charming and very successful at their work but their hearts are dead. A mate can try to squeeze some affection, a gentle touch, a kind look out of such a person and nothing will ever come. There are many of these walking dead among us, most of them are not just dead they are also continually enraged, and it's not so simple a matter to identify them on first sight, but they are there, prone to tempers, prone to violations of human decency and incapable of the emotions that direct most of us to reach out however clumsily for each other.

You wouldn't want such a person for your parent and you wouldn't want such a person for your spouse. But a lot of people have just that. Some people are so bad that others don't believe it even when they are told stories that leave no doubt. Some people are so bad that they simply can't be fixed and neither can the marriages they are in. When we watch television we see bad guys with guns who are criminals and we see good guys chasing them. We see sweet fellows in comedies who are trying to be good family men. We see bossy mothers-in-law or grouchy dads, cops with kid problems, women paramedics with difficult love lives, but what we rarely see is the real bad people who live with us and steal the sunlight from so many homes. We would not be entertained by that reality TV.

I've known a few of those bad people in my life, incurably bad people. I don't know anyone who murdered or created a situation in which the police had to be called. But I knew that my father carried a hate around that would erupt from time to time in name calling and other insulting raging words. I knew he was not touched by a child's hand in his or by his wife's desire to please him with a special birthday present. He had no soft spot for kittens or dogs or art or movies, or jokes. He had no God. He had no substitute for God. He did not believe in good works. He thought all his relatives and acquaintances were stupid fools. He told them so. He kept himself immaculate, perfectly pressed and groomed. He came and went like a black panther moving through his jungle at his own time controlled only by his whim. His eyes were like hard stones. He did not enjoy our stories.

We often think that love can move mountains and I suppose it can sometimes. But love is not effective against those truly without souls, the deeply damaged, the corrupted. It is naive and dangerous to think so. So anyone who tries to rescue through marriage those who are beyond rescue has jumped into the beast's cage and can't be surprised when he or she becomes lunch.

Most people do not marry truly bad people and they still have trouble. But their troubles, disappointed expectations, different ways of coping and loving, sexual mismatings, and all the plagues of commonplace unhappiness that affect our marriages are not usually in themselves hopeless, beyond the reach of therapist, religious counselor or even the partners' own good sense. But bad people, hopeless people, people so damaged they cannot love, these people exist. No one has counted them, but we know there are more of them than is good for us. So many that each generation produces more and more.

The question, the big question, is why do so many otherwise sane souls marry with such an unerring eye for disaster? There is of course the rescue fantasy in which we think we will find ourselves in reclaiming someone else. We think the hard drinker, the angry man or woman will melt in our arms and become transformed by our goodness. Behind that delusion lies another: we may really believe that only a damaged person whom we will serve dutifully would have us.

The word *self-esteem* is one to choke on. It has been debased by overuse and flattened like a pancake on a hot griddle. In what regard we hold ourselves, in what way we respect or do not respect our bodies, our minds, our deeds is so complicated, so mercurial, so subject to the outside weather conditions, inside hurricanes, that it is not possible to speak of a person's low self-esteem without reducing the complications of heart and mind to what has become a mental-health slogan hardly carrying any meaning at all and often used as a cudgel. On the other hand each soul does send off its own light and if that light is dimmed by past experience, if that soul is bent over in pain or fear, that too affects the destiny of that soul. There is no modern life without nicks and cuts in the self. There is no modern life that can be simply explained by taking the temperature of the self-esteem factor.

We may believe that we can satisfy our peculiar but human need to punish ourselves through such a marriage. When a parent has failed us in a major way we sometimes turn our anger on ourselves out of guilt. The noxious mixture of rage and guilt that is brewed in an unhappy childhood can lead us to arrange our adult lives so that happiness is out of the question and the terrible home in which we grew will be replicated in our adult lives. Whatever the reasons, we are, in so doing, complicit in our ruin and bear our share of the responsibility for what happens next. Fate, coincidence, buffet us here and there but in addition we seem to have an invisible radar that leads us to good or bad places, that rises from our experiences, that belies our innocence in all that we do or do not do.

Let the moral waters not be muddied by our partial and still primitive understandings of the human mind. Let us not excuse ourselves because of our childhood tragedies. We need our spines, upright and stiff. Some people are just bad people and if you marry one of them the only solution is to get out with your life and your children's lives.

The Chronic Miserable

A therapist friend leans over the dinner table and says to me, "I've had many patients come to me because they are unhappy in their marriages, in fact miserable in their marriages, but as we work together it becomes clear that they are miserable in and of themselves and would be miserable with or without this marriage."

These are people who suffer from such guilt, such competitive feelings, such anxiety, such rage, that who in particular they married hardly matters. If they had no mate the same unhappiness would fill their days and the same unhappiness would be there if they changed mates. What this means is that some people have inner wounds that can't be healed by the most loving of spouses. Some people are so damaged that if they are not fighting with their mates they are on the phone screaming at department stores or phone companies or wading through quarrels with their sisters or parents or bankers. Some people are so anxious and fearful that if they weren't refusing to go on a vacation with a spouse they would be refusing a friend's invitation to go to a movie. If they weren't drinking they'd be doing drugs and if they weren't abusing some substance they'd be threatening suicide and if they weren't threatening suicide they'd be harassing their coworkers or sleeping all day or driving like lunatics on our roads.

Some people who think they are in unhappy marriages are just in unhappy bodies. Good therapy offers a lifeline. But someone has to reach out and catch the line and hold on tight. That doesn't always happen. Therapy doesn't always work.

Thank God for legal divorce. Thank God that we get second chances and even third. Thank God that insight into one's self does help prevent the same mistake being made over and over again. And above all else thank God for the good marriages which do exist, exist all around us, and remind us that we do not have to be victims of our childhoods.

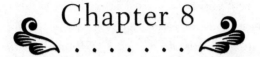

Chapter 8

To Honor and Obey

Here is the advice given to a young bride from a Yiddish work called "Lev Tov" ("A Good Heart") that was written in the early part of the seventeenth century by a Polish Jew and translated by Philip and Hanna Goodman in *The Jewish Marriage Anthology* (1965):

> *This is the story of a queen who gave her daughter in marriage to a young king and then gave her the following instructions. Take these ten rules to heart and think of them day and night and if you do this your husband will love you as he does the heart in his body.*
>
> *The first is to beware of his anger, lest you enrage him. When he is cross don't you be jolly and when he is jolly don't you be cross and when he is angry, smile at him and answer him with kind soft words—Search and consider about his food about that which he likes to eat—Try to have*

his meals ready at the proper time for hunger does nobody any good. Should he have gotten drunk, don't tell him what he said in his drunkenness and if he tells you to drink, you drink but don't drink yourself drunk, lest he should see you in such a state and learn to hate you. When he sleeps guard his sleep for if he doesn't get a good night's rest he may become very angry. Try to be thrifty and careful with your husband's money and make an effort not to bring any loss to him. Don't be anxious to know his secrets and if you should know anything of his secrets don't confide them to anyone in the whole world.

Find out whom he likes and like that person too, and him whom he dislikes, you dislike too. Don't like his enemies and don't hate his friends.

Do everything he tells you. If he tells you anything, let his words find favor with you. Don't say to him: You haven't said the right thing, or My advice is better than your advice.

Don't expect of him anything he considers difficult. He may take a dislike to you because you expect something of him which he believes is too hard.

Heed the requests which he may make of you, awaiting in turn that he will love you if you do so and will be your slave and will serve you with joy.

Be careful to guard against jealousy. Don't make him jealous in any way. Don't say anything that might hurt him and let him have his own way in everything. If you treat him like a king then he, in turn, will treat you like a queen.

Which goes to show that nothing is new under the sun and that Laura Doyle's book *The Surrendered Wife* is really an updated recycled message taught to a seventeenth-century Jewish bride in the heart of Eastern Europe.

The new style of marriage forged in the feminism of the 1960s has created a backlash or a backward slide among some of us. A popular book, *The Surrendered Wife* is proof positive that when a culture moves forward you can be sure someone is going to try to pull it back. We had Marabel Morgan's *The Total Woman* and endless lectures by Phyllis Schlafly and other conservatives who were afraid like Chicken Little that a woman in the workplace would make the sky fall down. *The Surrendered Wife* by Laura Doyle bills itself as "A practical guide to finding intimacy, passion and peace with your man." What this self-appointed guru is suggesting is that women stop using their brains and simply agree with everything that their husbands say or do. The book suggests that you don't correct mistakes, don't suggest ways to handle money, don't try to teach or improve him. Let him drive off the highway at the wrong exit. Let him make all vacation decisions. She claims that this passivity on the part of the woman will turn the husband into a passionate lover and a considerate partner. Since many women are afraid of losing their husbands, afraid of divorce and abandonment, this book speaks to their fears, promising if you give up your independence you will gain safety. But at a price (sacrifice of dignity, brains, energy, will) way too high for most women to consider. Even in the darkest prefeminist days men did not control their wives in this manner. There were always jokes about bossy women and submissive men. Consider Lady Macbeth for one. Consider Dagwood Bumstead and Lucy and Scarlett O'Hara. Consider all the jokes about controlling wives and the fact that women have exerted power through clever manipulation, through purse strings, through street smarts all along. The image of the docile wife who walks six steps behind her man and smiles sweetly at everything he does is an image as unreal as that of the darling baby who never throws a temper tantrum or wouldn't think of pushing his food onto the floor. Even women covered by the burqa must have their means of self-assertion and revenge. The queen mother quoted above instructing her daughter on her upcoming marriage clearly knew that her daughter would unless cautioned against it speak up, act out, assert herself. No one makes rules about things that people aren't tempted to do, aren't already doing. Dominance and submission have never been clearly cut on the gender axis. Marriage has always contained an element of struggle over control and no one knows exactly what goes on in anyone else's marriage. Weakness can be a kind of control. Bossiness can be an illusion. Feminism has simply created an equal playing field for the drama to unfold.

The Bible, emerging as it did from the patriarchal ancient world where the divisions of labor were clear and the role of women unquestioned encourages the orderliness of a hierarchical marriage. But modern life with its need for educated people who can be of either sex to enter the workplace, with its profound commitment to individual fulfillment and personal happiness, cannot take as gospel the Gospel texts that require female submission, not in an industrial, capitalistic, free-wheeling, say-everything, unmoored-from-ancient-traditions society such as ours. For better or worse no matter how many books advise to the contrary men and women are going to strive for an equal or dominant place in their marriages and the vast majority will pay no attention to the voices promising them happiness if only they would abandon their souls and surrender to the will of the other. Submission to the husband is an ideal that has long been honored only in the breach. We didn't need feminism to spark our independent thoughts, our desire to give advice, our independent judgment on people and events. And as for making the partner jealous this has been a factor in marriage ever since Abraham took Hagar for a mistress and Sarah grew green with envy.

The need to dominate women has its primal roots in the need to keep women from extramarital sexual encounters. In medieval Jewish life the wife was expected to cut off her hair and wear a wig so that other men would not desire her and lust after her because of her lovely locks and she would be marked as belonging to another. Muslims insist that their women cover their hair and sometimes their faces so no man may gaze on them. This is to insure the patriarchal line, to mark the child as one related to the father. It is also a primitive expression of male fear of female seductiveness as if the woman has some special power that needs to be hidden under black cloth, or mutilated with a shaved head. The roots of male patriarchal oppression lie in fear of female sexual power. Laura Doyle does not prescribe a particular haircut but her formulas for marital bliss require the same amputations of soul and inhibiting of personal style as carried by the custom of shearing the hair of the bride or covering her in black which is a metaphor for all the limitations of freedom to follow.

When women's awareness of male domination in the world at large came home to roost and American women were no longer so willing to follow men to their jobs across the country, to sacrifice their own opportunities for those of their mates, new kinds of trouble entered the home. As more and more women spoke out about physical abuse by their partners feminism made it clear that the culture was changing and women would no longer suffer in silence, without help at least from each other.

As more and more women kept their maiden names when they married and in so doing made a statement about the value of their individual uncoupled selves marriage itself became increasingly a partnership between two human beings of equal worth whether or not the woman stayed home to take care of the children. The demands of the feminist movement that domestic work be paid or valued equally with work outside the home were never met but they were heard and young men and women marrying today have very different expectations than those of their fathers or grandfathers. Let me do a small victory dance here.

This amounts to a revolution. Although today almost no one wants to be called a feminist almost every home in the Western world has been altered by the feminist vision, its power arrangements changed, its financial arrangements changed. Naturally enough there is a counterrevolution, a cry from those who liked it better the way it was, or think they did for religious, political reasons. The cultural wars in America between the conservatives and the rest of us center on issues that feminists raised.

Feminism may have urged a woman to become a neurosurgeon but it was never clearly explained to her what she may have to sacrifice to achieve this goal. Yes, this may be the unfortunate byproduct of women's equality but don't forget that before the women's movement had begun women suffered with a huge rate of depression, struggled with empty-nest misery, were often left widowed or divorced without a means to support themselves. The price women paid for enduring the traditional role in marriage was very high, hard on the intellect, hard on the spirit.

That the feminist vision did not bring universal happiness in its wake is not a reason to long for earlier times when things in fact for both men and women in marriages were far from ideal. Sadly enough we must acknowledge that happiness is as rare as it ever was. Female empty-nest depressions may be less frequent but depression itself has proved resilient to change. Prozac and Zoloft have replaced Miltown and Thorazine as the drugs of choice but the numbers of prescriptions floating about tell us that anxiety and sorrow afflicting both sexes will require more than a social revolution to leave us alone. For that we may have to wait for the coming of the Messiah.

The change in cultural style, the liberation of women from the routine domestic tasks, the act of parental sharing so many young couples engage in today has not made marriages a good deal more secure or satisfying than they were before. It certainly hasn't made them any worse. But the divorce rate continues to rain misery on our gardens and produce social confusion in all our heads.

I had great hopes for equality in marriage. I still believe it is the right form for any union to take but equality is only one of the factors in making a marriage a happy one and all is not well on the domestic front just because the form of the marriage has altered for the better. This is too bad. Feminism cured some ills but brought others down on our heads. This is the nature of social change.

You could, like certain radio talk-show hosts, point a finger at the feminist movement and blame it for all the divorces and loneliness we see around us. It is true that in the heady days of feminist discovery more women left their homes in pursuit of self-fulfillment than might have otherwise. In the wake of social change some marriages fell apart that might have been worth saving. It is true that women's drive for equal opportunity in the workplace, in the professions unleashed a host of accompanying demands. Men should wash their own socks, iron their own shirts, do the dishes and change the diapers. It is true that because of the feminist emphasis on work many women postponed marriage while they completed their education, an education all too quickly abandoned by previous generations in favor of marriage. It is true that unmarried women in their late thirties may now be sorry about their choices and fear they are too late to have children. Women who concentrated on their careers may have missed the family boat and while some may be pleased at this result most are grieved to the bone.

Male and Female
Created He What?

We still do not understand what it means to be a man or a woman and what precisely our sexual genitals have to do with our behavior in the real world. Having overthrown some of the stereotypes of earlier eras (female equals passive, male equals aggressive), we are not sure what we have left to define our roles and our natures. The old stereotypes and gender divisions are still hanging about our heads. They didn't just disappear or melt away in the 1970s. We are still puzzling over what it means to be masculine and what it means to be feminine, especially in a world where work may not mark the differences clearly. Animals that we are, we still are motivated by attraction between the sexes and that attraction does depend on biological hormonal and behavioral differences. So now we have a new kind of mass anxiety about maleness and femaleness that is hard to talk about and hard to resolve. No wonder so many people are reading *The Surrendered Wife,* which promises to answer these gender questions by simple fiat.

We have always had men who were more passive than active and women who were more dominant than submissive. Anxiety about this animates the extreme macho cultures around the world. Men are not so much afraid of women doing them harm as they are of the female passive voice inside themselves. We are all made up of both active and passive tendencies and this can be unnerving, scaring us into exaggerating one side or another of ourselves. In addition sexual fulfillment and sexual performance require an acceptance and clarity about our genders.

The explanation for the positive change in Laura Doyle's marriage may be that her husband was not sure of his inherent masculinity and only when his wife became a ridiculous stereotype of female response was he able to feel sufficiently unthreatened to become a protective and loving male, or so we gather from her report.

If this explanation is correct then Laura Doyle's husband, insecure in his masculine identity, needed a wife to play doormat in order to shore up his anxious and queasy male vigor. She did that for him but what she had to do then was to reject and repress the active side of herself, the open aggressive, energetic assertive aspects of her own personality. He, in turn, finally had to repress the more passive side of his own being, rejecting it because his wife found it unacceptable. This means then that both of them were forced to sacrifice parts of themselves and in so doing were diminished, half of what they might have been. He must always offer protection and control and she must always offer submission and passivity. Ugh. The couple becomes like those wooly mammoths frozen in ice blocks as the centuries pass. Each loses something.

And of course on her part it was dishonest, a manipulation, a scam. She doesn't really think he knows best or has the wisest head about finances. She pretends so in order to let him play his male role according to the stereotype. This stereotype goes on and on like the energizer bunny long after one might think the battery juice had been exhausted. In the end Laura Doyle is still pulling the strings or recharging the batteries although from behind the curtain not in front. If he buys it, all right, but he is still performing attached to his strings and it seems as if she has achieved the rather remarkable feat of turning a real boy into a puppet.

If women were really naturally submissive and men were gallant knights marriages would go more smoothly than they do. Men, Marlboro men, CEOs, soldiers and football players too have strong needs to be babies, petted, protected, nursed just as women do. Women have energy, active desires to assert themselves, to express their angers, to win in competition. They always have. The problem with the prefeminist culture is that it deemed deviant, called names anyone who broke the rigid rules of the assumed gender difference.

In the world of high society in New York City in the 1880s well-brought-up girls did not go to school. The Reverend Morgan Dix, rector of Trinity, declared that the education of women should be solely for womanly purposes, "in order to be to the man all that he needs." A woman should be a "moral lever" and her role in life was "to keep her home pure and sweet and to rule and govern it prudently." Then there was brilliant literary Edith Wharton stuffed into this mold so firmly she barely escaped with her life and her art intact. In a novel, *The Reckoning*, written in 1902 she writes a passage that stings with truth:

> *Her husband's personality seemed to be closing gradually in on her, obscuring the sky and cutting off the air, till she felt herself shut up among the decaying bodies of her starved hopes. A sense of having been decoyed by some world-old*

conspiracy into this bondage of body and soul filled her
with despair. If marriage was the slow life-long acquittal of
a debt contracted in ignorance, then marriage was a crime
against human nature.

This kind of marriage may well have been a crime against
human nature. One that made victims of many women. My
father, a lawyer, told me in the 1950s that women lawyers
were ugly, all of them, rejects from the marriage market that
no man would want to live with. He called my mother a stupid
dame, a dopey bitch. This was not said with affection. This
was not an accurate description of my mother. When a female
friend of the family wrote a play about to open on Broadway
my father called the playwright a stupid broad who could
never have written anything worthwhile. She had. Feminism
arose out of this culture of rejection of our minds and capabil-
ities. But it was never intended (except by a small minority) as
a rejection of our female sexuality or of masculine sexuality.
We believed that our sexual responsiveness and joy was connected to our female identity but just what compromised that
identity once you removed the barriers to an active life was not
clear. That's what future generations need to figure out.

Men staggered around under their own clichés which
pushed them into hiding their feelings, repressing their tears,
pretending to strengths they may not have had, into denying
their fears and losing touch with the gentler, needier aspects
of their personalities. Anyone who wants to send us back there
has a terminal case of nostalgia and ought to be quarantined
because such longing for an ideal of the past that was far less

than ideal is obviously contagious and presents a clear danger to the public health.

I have noticed that my daughter's generation is most comfortable with extremely feminine clothes, with heels that prevent running and styles that provide sexual attitude as well as seem to be open invitations. In the early days of feminism we thought clothes like that reduced us to sex objects. We were more puritan, more rejecting of feminine artifice. Ours was a reaction to bound feet and corseted bodies. Their costumes seem to be a reaction to our fear of our own sexual expression. So it goes. There is a courage and outspokenness in their dress that seem to be a way of answering a question: what is female if it isn't passive? Maybe this generation is on the way to a marriage that does not threaten the male and a masculinity that does not require suffocation of the female.

If the man changes the baby's diaper and shops for dinner and takes a turn at vacuuming the living-room rug can he still be the leader of the hunt, the protector of the hearth, the sexually attractive male figure of our dreams? If a woman earns a six figure salary and carries a briefcase can she still maintain the allure of femininity, can she still provide the warmth and sanctuary and sexual mystery the bedroom requires? We cannot lose all the boundaries between male and female and live in a completely washed-out desexed world without losing something of our biology, something in our most pleasurable flirtations and our most important seductiveness, and betraying our genuine erotic natures. At the same time we can't keep the old stereotypes as they were handed down to us through the ages without disappointing some of our expectations in each other, without spoiling something that still has value in our lives.

Our new marriages, in which both partners earn money and both partners nourish and nurture the children, are dancing around this problem. They have no other choice. No simple solution is to be found in any book or out of the mouth of any preacher, teacher or Ph.D. We are in this together and it is not simple.

In my first marriage the problem of gender role never came up. It was not around in the culture and we had no words to talk about it. We were dealing rather with the division between sane and insane, sober and drunk, wanting to parent, not wanting to parent. We could have exchanged genders and everything in our marriage been exactly the same as it was. I used him to satisfy my own ambitions but that cannot be exclusively female and is probably equally true of male spouses of writers, like Leonard Woolf, George Lewes, Louisa May Alcott's husband. My first husband did employ me to cook, wash sheets, scrub toilets. But he also used me to earn money and I served as breadwinner until the end of the marriage. Long before gender expectations were such an issue in marriage many people reversed the roles at least in part and many people ignored the rules and real life has never been as rigid as all that.

In my second marriage, which unfolded at the same time as the feminist movement in America, my husband and I bumbled our way to a life in which gender still matters a lot but limits neither of us to a narrow place. He drives. I am the passenger. He pays the check at the restaurant. I smile at the waiter. He pays the taxes and is the steadier wage earner but we both work. I arrange to meet our friends and he cooks dinner for them. He gardens and I do laundry. He is silent and I am a constant communicator. He is not alarmed by the winds that come and go and I am always expecting a hurricane. In times of disaster he is tight but calm. In times of disaster I am teary and terrified and only stop talking to sleep. He would kill anyone who would try to harm me or our children. I would run for the police or hide in a closet. I like the fact that he was a soldier and I like the fact that he knows how to walk a colicky baby until its pain eases. I can see the remnants of sexual stereotypes in our marriage in each of our behaviors. Are they there because we were raised with them or are they there because we chose them, or because they can never be eradicated without harm to our sexual union? I'm not sure. I don't think anybody is.

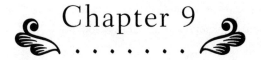

Chapter 9

The Overly Loud, Unnecessarily Smug Outcry Against the Nontraditional Home

These days a woman who wants a baby but has not been able to find a suitable mate is able to raise a child and love a child anyway. These days women who love women and men who love men can also raise children, wash their ears, see to their homework, plan birthday parties, worry about the future like the rest of us. This is a good thing. It should not make us anxious that human love, adult for child, has expanded and exploded outside of the conventional lines. Single parenthood, something conservatives consider as a way of dancing with the devil, is a possibility eagerly seized by many women without partners who are coming to the end of their fertility. Single parenthood is a second-best choice, providing a home resting on one-half a foundation. No doubt, however, that a second-best choice may be far better than the third choice of not raising a child at all. Everyone's life is made up of many second-best choices or third. A single mother may do far better with a child than a married teenage mother or a married mother who is unhappy in her marriage or with her lot in life. We are a very judgmental society and are always looking to find someone else in mortal error.

There are so many factors that make it possible to raise a child well, some of them in the child himself or herself, that the lack of a father or a mother in the enterprise cannot be the great dividing line between good and bad parenting. Nature gives us other handicaps—blindness, deafness, prematurity, and learning problems are just a few among the long list of potential afflictions. Depression in a parent, addictions, economic failure, chronic illnesses of all sorts make it hard for children in any given home. And then there are the subtler problems of bad tempers, neurotic fears, inhibitions, obsessions that can darken any home, one parent or two.

We worry too much or about the wrong things or our worry is prompted by the remnants of a puritanical morality that tyrannized us for so long. All through history early death made many families change their shapes and forms. When women died in childbirth, when a man could die from stepping on a rusty nail or contracting a bad cold many children were without one or another or both parents. This was not good but it did not mean the end of the world. Substitutes, stepparents, schools, churches, aunts and uncles were often able to step in and provide the nourishment that children need. Put in perspective the alarming family statistics we see today are not cataclysmic at all. Remember Hester and Pearl who stood above the crowd in every way that really matters.

My father had an illegitimate son with his mistress. After my mother died he married the boy's mother and took the boy, then twelve, into his home. What was sad about this was that another man lost his wife and a child he thought was his. The other children in that family lost their home. What was sad about this is that my father betrayed my mother. What was sad about this is that he preferred his second son to his first, my brother. What makes for complicated hard feelings here is that my father kept his sexual affairs a secret while behaving in an unloving way to his wife and his children. Our legitimacy was of no emotional use to us in gaining his affection, which was the more important matter.

We may not need marriage to have children. We do not need marriage to make our children acceptable in the best schools, in the best homes, in the finest clubs. It is true that marriage today carries with it a high risk of failure and children of divorced parents may be especially leery of exploring a country from which their own parents may not have escaped with their skins.

The dumbest bumpkin knows it, there is no emotional hedge fund to protect you if your marriage flounders downward.

I would be a single mother in a heartbeat if my life had brought me into my late thirties without a mate. Granted some handicap, there are risks worth taking. If I could support myself and a baby I would do so by any reasonable means at hand. I would never get married to make the sociologists or the church people happy. I would never feel guilty that I was an outlaw in a moral society. I know that morality is not in a license issued by a state or a church but dwells rather in each of us and our intimate relationships and is revealed in the way we love and care for one another. Above everything else I would never accept a life without motherhood because I had trouble finding a lifetime mate. Never.

The gay and lesbian home that raises children either through conception or adoption is simply in for a slightly different set of complications. These will be no better or worse than those in more conventional homes. It seems strange to me that anyone would like to prevent anyone else from giving a child a roof over his or her head. Why would anyone not want a child to have a holiday tradition, a parent to protect him or her, a parent to radiate pride, to urge onward, a home as a source of comfort and a place to grow? That homes can be created with two mommies or two daddies seems simply to broaden the possibilities, increase the number of hearths at work. Why would anyone think our world would be better if wanted children were left unborn and unwanted children unadopted? If, knowing all the obvious drawbacks and dangerous pitfalls of traditional married life, gay and lesbian couples want to join the barn raising, my only sorrow would be that happily ever after remains a sometime thing no matter the gender choice of the two adults who will pledge their troth to each other.

Two Cheers
for the Arranged Marriage

I wonder why it is that educated women, competent women, anxious to love and anxious to live in a family, to bear and raise children, are having such a hard time finding that mate. Why are all those biological clocks ticking away in so many disconsolate hearts? What is wrong that with all the singles ads, with all the matchmakers, mothers and fathers, aunts and uncles, offices and classes, resorts and dating services, that so many women and men still roam around without making it to the altar, at least not in time to satisfy biological clocks? We believe in romantic love. We believe there is a Mr. or Mrs. Right out there around the corner. But we know the system isn't working well, not for so many, not now. Are we now at a point where marriage lacks any allure, any necessity, any reason for continuing its presence among us? In other cultures, Pakistan, China, Tibet, divorce is less common, less possible, less likely. In other places, India, Uzbekistan, Syria, marriage is arranged by the parents with minimal consent by the children. These arranged marriages are not based on what we would call free choice, deep love, expectations of romance. Since the man and wife get to know each other only after the wedding ceremony as they begin their lives together, the result, a happy companionship for man and woman, a friendship growing richer with the years, is settled by a hard spin on the wheel of fortune. I would assume, and this is just a commonsense observation based on a hunch, that these marriages, formed openly on class, status, wealth, family connections, do just about as well in the long run as ours. They could hardly do worse. These traditional societies do not have women in their thirties in singles bars hoping to find a mate. Men and women do not suffer from problems of commitment, midlife crisis, are not forced to put ads in the newspapers seeking mates. If there were a way to measure a society's loneliness factor like the pollen count in the air we might find the Western way up at unacceptable levels. If we could measure happiness in marriage we might find no statistical difference between those marriages made by free and independent choice and those planned by parents.

An American law professor tells of visiting a former female student of his from India who is now working at a prominent law firm in New Delhi. She tells him that her parents have begun the search and will soon arrange a marriage for her. He asks her why after so many years in America she is allowing them to select her husband. "Oh," she shrugs, "I am so busy. I work so late and on weekends. I have no time to do this myself." In America where arranged marriages are looked on as a form of indentured servitude this young lawyer would have to fend for herself and God help her out there, she would need the kind hand of providence.

Now that I'm a parent I'm even more tempted by the idea of the arranged marriage. How well I could do it. How easily I could protect my children from disastrous choices. How wise I am and how foolish they may be is quite clear at least to me. Who knows my children better than I, who could plan their future with more success? Who knows life and what it brings better, me or them? What a delicious if slightly pointless fantasy this is!

I know there are other problems. In the provinces of India young women are sometimes set afire if they do not please or the bride price is not met. In many such places wives are considered chattel and are kept inside the house with no hope of escape, distraction, affection. They may be married off by eager or greedy fathers to old men or wicked men or prevented from seeing their own families ever again. The horror stories are endless. Both sexes can easily end up bored, isolated, and more alone than if they were not married. However in those cultures "Ally McBeal" would fall right off the TV ratings scale. That is a mighty thing to contemplate. "Sex in the City" would make no sense in a culture where women were married young and had a houseful of children at Carrie's age. Those women whose marriages have been arranged don't have time to hallucinate little babies they're too busy tending, cleaning, birthing, etc. Adult women in their twenties would not be floundering from one live-in boyfriend to the next eating out of plastic plates as if life were an eternal stay in a college dorm. Women married in their teens are more apt to be naturally fertile so in vitro and a playground filled with twins would be as rare as a morning coat or a calling card today. No psychiatrist would hear the familiar words, "Why do I always pick the wrong man?" "Let's talk about that, shall we?" might become a statement as dated as "Hitch up the horses, we are going to a quilting bee." Freedom like everything else costs something and the price is very high.

In Jewish ultraorthodox cultures the father of the bride con-
tacts the father of the potential groom. A date between the
young people is arranged. They meet in a public place. If they
like what they see they can arrange another meeting. After a
few of these meetings a decision must be made. Either male
or female may back out. If they don't they're on their way to
their wedding. This plan doesn't allow for any sexual explo-
ration. This courtship under the ferns of a hotel plant is so
brief as to be no more than a physical checkout. The truly
repulsive are at a disadvantage while the emotionally shallow,
callow, obsessive, anxious, weird, or plain crazy are at an
advantage, since for a few hours almost anyone's less attractive
side can be kept under wraps.

The good part of this arrangement is that the culture, religious belief, way of life, expectations of both participants will
be the same. They don't have to take three dates to ask if the
other wants children, would be willing to send the children to
a religious school, etc. The woman does not have to worry that
the man has no means of supporting her. That will have been
checked out by her father. The man doesn't have to worry that
the girl is not of good reputation, hasn't had exactly the education or lack of it he would desire in a wife, doesn't know what
would be required of her as his wife. This all helps. Of course
the list of things they don't know about each other is far
longer. Does he like music? Does she hate her sister? Does he
lie and cheat in business? Does she love clothes or is she more
interested in politics than is proper? Is he a leader or a fol-
lower? Will she respect his mind? Will he respect and admire
hers or will he resent her opinions? What opinions does she

have anyway? Is he afraid of the dark like a baby? Has she the strength to take care of child after child as expected? Does she laugh a lot or is she surly? Is he brave or is he the kind who hides in order to avoid trouble? What is she like with a bad cold in her head? Does she snap at those around her? What is he like when he is defeated? Does he grow depressed for months on end or will he bounce back and try again? All these questions and many many more are only answered when a couple can live together some years before marriage or at least they might be.

In the Middle Ages in many parts of Eastern Europe the Jewish groom and bride did not meet before the wedding, not ever. There is a custom at the wedding where the bride and bridegroom after the blessings have been said are taken to a private place and given a short time to be with each other, to eat some food together. Here it was often that a groom could look on the face of his life's companion for the first time and she could gaze at him. Think of the power of that moment. Think of how much depended on their response to each other. What terror and hope, what sweetness and fear must have joined the couple in this private meeting. The families and the community have danced, have celebrated, will celebrate some more, the public part of the wedding is going on while the couple sit together privately beside each other in their wedding finery, passing cake and fruit back and forth. They have been told they should feed one another. She opens her mouth. He sees inside it, pink flesh. His heart thumps. He opens his mouth, she picks up the fork, she places it between his lips. These are the lips of a stranger. How odd, how frightening to be so close to a stranger and know that you must stay by his side ever after.

Think then of our contemporary wedding in which the bride and groom have shared a bathroom and a suitcase and his old sofa that his mother gave him for his graduate school dorm for a long time. Her underpants have slipped under a cushion. His jogging socks are in her laundry bag. They come to the wedding night with no trepidation. Nothing left to discover. He knows she has a mole beneath her right breast. She knows he has a scar on his shin from when he played ice hockey. She knows what he is afraid of and she knows what he wants of her. Why then does it still happen that after the wedding the couple discovers that in some way they were fooled, or misled, or didn't see some crucial matter that may in fact lead to divorce? Why does all that foreknowledge not protect us from disappointment? There is no mystery here. We simply do not always want for ourselves what we ought to have. We make choices that are destructive, impossible. If we are led by our crooked unconscious we may marry in search of misery and find it. Knowing is no protection against our dark sides.

Here is Anthony Trollope writing in his novel *Can You Forgive Her?*

> *Marrying people are cautioned that there are many who marry in haste and repent at leisure. I am not sure, however, that marriage may not be pondered over too much; nor do I feel certain that the leisurely repentance does not as often follow the leisurely marriages as it does the rapid ones. That some repent no one can doubt; but I am inclined to*

believe that most men and women take their lots as they find them, marrying as the birds do by force of nature, and going on with their mates with a general, though not perhaps an undisturbed satisfaction. . . . I do not know that a woman can assure to herself, by her own prudence and taste, a good husband any more than she can add two cubits to her stature; but husbands have been made to be decently good—and wives too, for the most part, in our country— so that the thing does not require quite so much thinking as some people say.

What would this sensible man have to say about years of premarital cohabitation?

The full impact of our power struggles, of our memories, of our ways of hiding and revealing ourselves does not seem to reveal itself until a legal marriage is underway. It is not that modern men and women are feckless or reckless in their choices. Their desire to live happily ever after is genuine and sincere. It's just that freedom of choice is not the same as a better choice.

Nevertheless, I do not or at least not very often envy other worlds their way of mating and procreating. I have treasured my own freedom to marry as I pleased and my children's freedom to make their own mistakes, to find their own way. I simply wish with all my heart that it was easier, the path more certain, the hill less steep. I only wish that freedom was not such a snake, biting friend and foe alike.

It was in the early 1600s that the idea of love and free choice in marriage began to spread. When Benjamin Franklin writing in 1743 made the point clear he was not expressing a revolutionary idea but one that was not yet universally accepted. He said,

> *No parental authority, thus to make us unhappy, that is repugnant to the dictates of reason and virtue or the moral happiness of our natures is anyway binding on children. To marry without a union of minds, a sympathy of affections, a mutual esteem and friendship for each other is contrary to reason and virtue. . . . It follows that no parental authority to make us unhappy by marriage is binding on children.*

If it were only the bad choice of parents that made marriages unhappy all would be well.

Franklin, writing in a time when America itself was preparing its soul for independence from the parent country, when the choice and freedom of individuals to worship, to choose how and where to live was highly prized in this new and open society, could never have imagined the hollow if not ironic tones these high-minded, moral-sounding words would have for twenty-first century listeners.

Because quite simply we can make ourselves unhappy without any help from our parents. Our freedom of choice sets us loose in a bewildering herd of our contemporaries. We may be looking for someone to set our bodies vibrating, someone we believe has a soul that will cherish our soul, that is like our soul, but are we right or are we wrong in our choice? The stakes are high. We may want someone as unlike our parents as we can find, a man who doesn't drink, who is better educated than our own daddy, who can offer us a passport into a higher station of life—that in fact is what Emma Bovary wanted and did not get. But what we want may not be the kind of thing we need. Or what we need may not be the thing we want. Once superficial beauty has lost its wonder have we chosen a shrew, a weak sister, a man without strength, a man or a woman incapable of coming close, leaning against, letting the partner into the dark places of the mind? If we have made a mistake like so many others around us what are the consequences of leaving this man or woman? Will we be lonely ever after?

Now if I could choose a mate for my daughters I would pick a son from the crop produced by friends or colleagues or neighbors of ours. That's the traditional way of doing it. How nice it would be if the family could have holidays all together. We would of necessity appreciate the political, religious convictions that had surrounded the young man. We would know what they were. He would have our attitudes towards everything from mayoral candidates to toilet training. He would like to vacation by the beach as his parents did, as we did. He would be ambitious and sane because we would weed out the dead heads, the pot heads, the animal-rights activists. On the other hand he wouldn't be an excessive risk taker. We would eliminate mountain climbers, bungee jumpers and day traders. We would eliminate any young man who was only interested in the size of his bank account. On the other hand we would eliminate any young man who thought he could make a living writing poetry and selling it in the subway. We would accept a painter but I wouldn't be above hoping his trust fund was adequate. We would rule out men with recorded bankruptcies, chronic skin disorders, claustrophobia, and illiteracy (that includes those reading only the sports pages) and those with acute panic attacks and those who have spent time in mental hospitals for bipolar disorders. Those illnesses and others may and in all likelihood will come later but no sense in starting out knowing the exact name of the trouble to come. I would, I admit, be concerned by a son of a mother who had been a suicide or one who had been raised in a Rumanian orphanage. I don't want my daughters' husbands to have had childhoods of such deprivation and sadness that it will take them fifty years to regain their optimism, to find their footing.

Ah, and then I would want to select a young man who would be able to improve on our way of doing things. I would hope the children of this couple would be free of some of the tugs and strains that affected our home. I want progress. I want happier and healthier grandchildren than any generation has produced up to this point. I want them secure in their identities. I want them brave and without the anxieties that give nightmares. I want them to venture forth where we were timid and to include in their lives traditions, cultures, adventures that were just beyond our ken. If I could find such a man I would arrange the match immediately.

But how would I make my daughter love, romantically love my choice? There is the rub. Having let the idea of love and free choice out of the bag how can we put it back in? It's such a powerful idea, this romantic notion of love, that no matter how foolish it has proved itself, it has staying power. It will not be reversed. So how then could I make my daughters accept my choice? I can't. Instead of my daughters accepting my selections I will as graciously as possible accept theirs. If they make one at all.

In countries where marriages are arranged the couples if they are lucky will find themselves friends and partners and maybe love will come in the day-to-day living that follows. Certainly it is hard not to love (if not in the heady sense, in the deep friendship sense) the person whose bed you share, who knows your body, who is the father or mother of your child. The situation calls for closeness. The arranged marriage may end up exactly as the chosen marriage, good or bad, depending on the character of the participants and the good fortune or bad fortune that life brings them.

How can I so easily dismiss the idea of romantic love? This idea has lit up the passions for centuries of Western history. It is the fire that sparks the plots of our greatest stories, from *Romeo and Juliet* to *Pride and Prejudice, Cyrano de Bergerac, Death in Venice*. A person can hardly read a thing, go to the theater, attend an opera without falling into star-crossed lovers working their way towards each other, whether it be comedy or tragedy. The scandal pages of the tabloids tell us movie stars are always falling in and out of love. That becomes part of their glamour, their power. From the fourteenth-century troubadours wooing their fine ladies in their castles to rock-and-roll lyrics dedicated to the singer's girl, or Patsy Kline and all of Nashville being jilted yet again, we have a long culture that recognizes the validity, the importance of up-close and very personal love. Love creates endless trouble and pain for human beings but incites them to say their best lines, to do heroic things. What kind of wet blanket would wish romantic love away from our lives?

A realist that's who. The word *love* is one we all respond to. We recognize it. We've been there. I don't have to explain when I tell my best friend I'm in love. The feeling is beyond ordinary language and only the best of poets approach it and even they can fall on their faces when talking about love. Still we think we understand what we mean by love. But we don't. Love is a word that can hide all sorts of misfortunes. Love is what the woman feels for the man who abuses her. She has always loved him and is so grateful when he smiles at her. This is love with a masochistic sheen. On the surface it looks sweet. Underneath it is all purple with bruises. When my daughters have been about to break up with a boyfriend I always hear about how much they love him. They don't seem to know that they are angry at him, tired of him, bored by him, insulted by him or whatever has caused the drifting apart. They only know that their hearts are broken, they really love him.

I was sick with love for my first husband for months after we separated and it took years before I could hear his name without a surge of emotions, mixed emotions of course, battering my nerves. Love is what we feel when we may need so badly that we can't stand on two feet without being propped up by another. Love is what we may feel when we grow attached to someone we want to control, to humiliate, to demolish. Love is so easily transformed into obsession, desperate need, fixation on the presence of another. When this happens we are less involved with the real object of our hearts and more involved in some primitive drama (will mother come back, will Daddy choose me over my sister?). If this person loves me I may avoid death, absorb his or her youth, take on his or her qualities which are lacking in me. Obsession is the hand that fits into the glove of love. This has little to do with the purposes of marriage and argues for the safety of the arranged marriage where obsession is kept out of the matter and the selection of the mate is made on more practical grounds.

We ourselves most often don't know what lies behind our own loving emotions but the simple valentine (all roses and chocolates) will often serve like a Band-Aid on a gushing wound. Love may be mingled inextricably with hate. When love is obsessive there is certainly an element of rage in its ferocity. Love is dangerous because it beckons us near but can do us harm, mean us harm.

When we love we become dependent on our love. This can make us angry and cause us to behave badly when our lover surprises us by being someone other than we expected.

We all want to love. It sounds so good. Here is the disaffected Flaubert on Emma Bovary some months after her marriage to Charles. "Before she had married she thought she was in love. But the happiness that should have resulted from this love had not come: she must have deceived herself, she thought. Emma sought to learn what was really meant in life by the words, 'happiness,' 'passion,' and 'intoxication'—words that had seemed so beautiful to her in books." Emma chases passion the way some men chase money and she finds that she has manufactured the emotion from her own brain, that it has led her into disappointment and debt. She cannot hold on to the intensity of the feeling she seeks any more than one can grasp a sunbeam and place it in a frying pan. In Emma's limited mind the idea of love hid her own selfishness and incapacity to love. It covered with grand plans her paucity of tenderness, her willingness to betray even her own child. The tragedy was not so much that the men she chose to fill her empty soul proved disappointing but that her soul was so scheming, petty and small to start with.

But we cannot banish romantic love any more than we can rid our culture of drugs or alcohol or X-rated movies. It is an opiate of the soul and beyond government intervention. All we can do is recognize that love is a hydra-headed monster and should be approached with caution, which alas is exactly what is thrown to the winds when love enters. In America where today free choice is the rule in affairs of the heart and is supposed to be the only legitimate reason for a marriage we speak of love in simple terms but endure all its ravages, its hidden meanings, its habit of so frequently savaging our happiness.

Bridget Jones, the heroine of a British best-seller by Helen Fielding now known around the world, squirmed away from her mother's selection of a prominent lawyer whose family had known her family all of her life, had seen her in fact running naked on their lawn. But in the end she found out that mother was right and that the selected mate was the right mate who would make her happy. The moral, as noted by Bridget herself at the happy ending of this modern fairy tale, is that one should "do as your mother tells you."

I really like this idea. *Bridget Jones's Diary* may be a great book. It should become a classic, something like *The Iliad* for modern times.

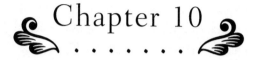

Chapter 10

On the Good Ship Courtship
Things Are Not So Shipshape

It's no secret that the age of first marriage, after a remarkable low in the 1950s, is rising on the tide of female education and opportunity. In many parts of educated America that age creep has pushed up into the thirties. Since these figures are averages we could probably count in the millions the unmarried singles who are well into their adulthood. Listen carefully and you can hear the collective biological clock ominously ticking away. There is massive and painful anxiety across the land as women race to the finish line, by then weary and bruised by breakups and disappointments and wised up (if not wise) due to less than perfect experiences. Innocence is not a quality we see in most brides these days.

The desire to have a family, to be loved by and to love one man, to share life with one spirit, has not disappeared with "Ozzie and Harriet," "Leave It to Beaver," "Blondie and

Dagwood" and the rest of the gang. It's just a goal that seems harder and harder to achieve. Well yes, if you miss the mating season in college then you have another chance in your early twenties and if you made a mistake in your twenties or a series of mistakes you always have another chance because every man is not taken, someone else's mistake is your very own heart's desire. But the field does narrow. Many more men are gay than women. Many more men who have no biological time limitations and may or may not have raising children on their immediate agendas are holding back, not committing, playing the field. More and more children of divorce regard the prospect of married life with a jaundiced eye and an athlete's fleet foot. And men of course, whom society has given the unjust edge, have open to them the newest crop of ever younger women which increases their pool and shrinks a woman's in one cruel stroke. The fact that men can choose from crops of ever younger females is a hangover from our bad old days in which men had all the real power and women held only the short-lived beauty card. This advantage for the male is also a product of our biology, which permits fatherhood forever down the life span thus making the fertile woman available to the older man and permitting him all the pleasures that her flesh can offer. Her bloom carries with it a promise of reproduction that heightens the attraction and sets his hormones as well as hers to dancing in the air. This is not just but it is so.

This is the stuff in women's magazine editors who will, in order to sell their wares, remain upbeat. If you just change your hair color or vacation in the Bahamas or lose those last ten pounds then all will be well. Bridget Jones was herself a great believer in the elusive goal of weight loss. But the truth is that once past thirty a woman worries and she worries with good reason. If she lets her worry show she will be surely shunned. What is less appealing than a desperate woman on the hunt? Perhaps a dead rat in your bed? If she puts her head in the sand and takes no steps to find a mate then she may well remain a loser in what she may believe is the most important game of her life.

We used to think that men felt trapped by marriage, that their sex urges raged like out-of-control brush fires. All the jokes of the fifties were about women trying to tie men down and men whispering about a freedom they had lost. How else to explain the bachelor parties with naked girls jumping out of cakes? But that itself is fallout from a patriarchal system that is no longer with us, at least not in the same ways or with the same power to control our lives. These days we know that sex urges are distributed equally to all the genders, male and female and in-between. Bachelorette parties complete with sex toys are held across the land. We know that men are as eager and needy of partners as women and that a lonely man is as sad a sight as a lonely woman.

No one would deny that luck may play a part in this courtship ritual. The right man may just take an apartment next door to the right woman and they will meet in the elevator and get married eleven months later. The right woman may be your best friend's sister and as soon as she returns from designing a hotel in Malaysia she has dinner with you and the rest is a story to tell the children.

But for most of us luck is made and bad luck is constructed out of our own errors of judgment and character which do in turn carry our pasts in all their parts. For most of us the right man is the man whom we have actually met and are able to love. We can adjust our sharp edges to his sharp edges. For most of us the right man is not only the one we happened to meet but the one we happened to meet when we were ready. Ready means that we were done trying to harm ourselves or soothe some inexplicable guilt. Ready is not luck or good fortune. Ready is earned by life experience or ready is a gift granted by a childhood free of misery: a rare thing in this world indeed.

So the mistakes people make in their twenties are not random or not as random as we would hope. Someone is always attracted to men who fail at whatever they do. Someone else gets involved with men who can't love or won't love. Someone else clings so tight to anyone who approaches that they run away instantly. Someone else is so afraid of being wounded that they never allow anyone near enough for a spark to ignite, for a fire to blaze. The list of ways in which we can sabotage ourselves is endless and this is an equal opportunity problem. Men too may find themselves again and again having found a woman who seems to need protection but who then drains them of every ounce of energy as she threatens to sink under the strain of living. Men may find themselves rejected by women who will not love or trust another being. Men too risk all when they go out courting and they too make mistakes that chip away at their confidence, are time consuming and leave them wondering if ever someone just right will come along.

These days some of the decorative feathers that men traditionally flounced in courtship have lost their worth on the open market. Now that women too earn money and have careers, simply being able to provide is not as compelling an asset as it once was. That a man can cook or announces that he is willing to change diapers is an essential but does not necessarily increase his sex appeal to the lady he is trying to win. We are all so mixed up about what is sexy in men and what is sexy in women and how that relates to the bad old gender roles that we are thankfully rid of, that the task of attraction is complicated. A man who is a real warrior might want a woman who admires him and tends the hearth but what if she is a warrior too? A man should be a good competitor in our competitive world but what if the woman is a competitor also? How can they keep from competing with each other? Do the potential mates spur each other on or do they knock each other down? What happens to a man when his helpmeet earns more than he does? Is a successful woman a marked lady or is she walking around with an ace in her sleeve? There is a muddle out there and it makes the process of dating and loving and trusting and marrying even more complicated than it was when romantic love and free choice were first introduced in the early seventeenth century.

In the wild days of the sexual revolution it seemed as if men and women might not need a lifetime partner after all. Everything about traditional marriage seemed old-fashioned, uncool, and even dangerous to your mental health. This was the hype. It was not what most real people believed or acted upon. Singleness, despite granting freedom from compromise, freedom from bother, freedom from financial and emotional responsibility, is obviously not an entirely comfortable condition. It may be that we need a mate in order to feel safe, sound, anchored. It may be that we look for love out of some dreamy dream of being folded into another, happily ever after.

It is true that marriage can leave you miserable and a bad marriage is like being boiled alive every day but the lack of marriage, the lack of opportunity to raise children makes people sad, the vision of lost connection haunts, it is hard to laugh bravely when in your late thirties you see your prospects disappearing and you think of yourself as a person who has to cry on your own shoulder or market for one ever after. Here is a woman over thirty as reported in Helen Fielding's *Bridget Jones's Diary.* She says, "As women glide from their twenties to thirties—the balance of power subtly shifts. Even the most outrageous minxes lose their nerve, wrestling with the first twinges of existential angst: fears of dying alone and being found three weeks later half-eaten by an Alsatian."

The fascination with *Bridget Jones's Diary* and the sit-coms "Sex in the City" and "Ally McBeal" tells us that the single thirty-something woman longing for a mate has pierced into the heart of the current cultural ache just the way that the little tramp eating his own shoe was a joke that was not a joke for its own hard times. Chaplin was pushed and pulled around the assembly line like an object being mauled by the impersonal, new-for-its-time technology and most people found his misery funny, just as today we enjoy the endless inevitable disappointments of Carrie or Ally or Bridget in their search for the holy grail of a true love. Good comedy is always based on a tragic reality.

But men too want to find love or romance, look for a partner, want to be fathers whether it is exactly like or exactly unlike their own fathers. The male animal has the same reproductive urge that overcomes the female of the species. He too when he leaves this earth wants to leave his genes behind, become a parent and grandparent. Not all men of course, not all women either, but in the main, men do not like eating take-out food, playing games with bodies to which they have no emotional connection, trying endlessly to find such a connection at a bar or a party or on a blind date. There is the same desperation in the man who has failed to find someone as there is in the woman. He too is lonely, feels left out at gatherings of his married friends. He too has a few battle stories to tell, and while his biological clock may purr happily rather than tick ominously he too realizes that he is missing something, something he can't seem to find.

Think of the mail-order brides from the Philippines or Russia who even in today's world list themselves in catalogs and are shipped like so many pounds of herring from one continent to another. This is not because the men can't find sex without a catalog. They can, brothels, bars, and women who are loose from their moorings, wild women, damaged women, runaway girls have always been available. Now we add to this pool the divorced woman and the single woman who is looking for a mate or a good time or the married woman who is ready for something else on the side. Post–sexual revolution

men don't need mail-order brides for sex. The continued traffic in mail-order brides exists because some men can't seem
to find a local woman to marry them, bear their children, hold
their heads when they are ill, whisper their names in the dark
of the night.

What kind of a man can't find a woman to marry him in a
world where so many women can't seem to find men to marry?
There is no measurement, no poll that can give us the statistics on the many ways we can be peculiar, odd, unacceptable
to others, overweening in our demands, frightening in our sexual habits, pale in the impression we leave on others. We all
learned in grade school that some people are outside the
magic circle of normality. In every class all the children know
the names of the losers and nerds and outsiders. These are the
subtly odd as well as the withdrawn or socially clumsy or
excessively shy or intensely nervous boys and girls. There are
those with physical abnormalities that make them seem like
strangers who deserve to be eaten by the pack. Those who
stutter, those who are tiny or too tall, those who don't catch on
to the joke or can't keep up with the patter. There are those
who are caught in their own fantasies and those who have
already gone dead in the eyes. They may finally make it into a
job that suits them or a profession in which they excel but they
don't make it across the room to ask a girl to dance, and no one
wants to go home with them.

Judging from the success of the mail-order bride business,
there are a lot of those men who nevertheless want to be married, who want to have children and families. And why should-
n't they by whatever means they can?

The mail-ordered women of course have economic reasons, or green-card reasons or simply think everything American will produce bliss ever after. They too are ones who couldn't or didn't link up with men in their own community. Perhaps they were too ambitious or too cold or too shy or too poor or crippled in body or in mind. Perhaps they simply became too long in the tooth for the men of the neighborhood or ruined their reputations or are escaping prison. Why shouldn't they take a chance on a man who seems to offer, at least on paper, a life better than the one they have?

Look how hard people try to get married. Since there is no great matchmaker in the sky perhaps we can develop a department in the university that teaches the skill, credits in psychology accepted, a degree presented and a professional roster of licensed matchmakers available to all and as welcome in their neighborhoods as dentists and men of the cloth.

Today men who are not priests sworn to celibacy or pedophiles leering into the blue light of their computers while the rest of the world sleeps, look to marriage for exactly the same reasons that women do, sexual pleasure mingled with companionship, friendship that will last a lifetime through, parenthood, which many feel is both their way of being blessed and of blessing the world around them. So why is it so hard these days for so many to find a mate?

Bridget Jones tells us that many men suffer from what she calls "emotional fuckwittage." That is to say, they like sex but have little patience or desire for any of the things that occur out of bed. They enjoy seduction but have no interest in responsibility, faithfulness, fatherhood, or a long walk along a lakeside talking about childhoods and school-days and old wounds and bad movies they loved as well as fears of flying or spiders or bridges, reporting on jobs lost and languages unlearned and friends who are no longer friends, things that are not part of the seduction process but absolutely essential to the knowing, the real knowing of another.

One has to wonder why this plague of infantile males seems to have hit our urban centers, if it actually has. Is this some collective male revenge for women's upsetting the balance of power as it had existed for so long? More probably the male who flees a real woman's hand on his arm has been damaged long ago by a mother or a father or invading hordes of barbarians and now his heart has broken and he is afraid to trust or love without assuring himself of an escape route. This focus on the escape can limit how far a man can go towards a woman. But what is it such men really fear and what has happened to them?

Maybe this "fuckwittage" is nothing new. It seems counter to common sense that suddenly at the end of one century and the beginning of another men should become cads in such large numbers simply because they can. What has changed in this postfeminist and post–sexual revolution universe is that men can be themselves without pretense, without marrying and making some woman miserable by cheating on her endlessly. Have the numbers of unsuitable boys actually increased or have they (which seems more likely) simply come out of their hiding places to play in the sunlight?

Before the recent women's movement male superiority and dominance was taken for granted and masculinity was illustrated by the sexual possession of a woman. Now that the sexual act no longer guarantees male dominance and masculinity itself is hard to define we may have an increased batch of men whose masculinity remains childlike, intent on instant gratification. These men are not sure of themselves as males and can be very easily shaken when real demands are made on them. It may be that not loving and not committing to a relationship is some men's way of assuring themselves of their maleness by leaving themselves free to play in an endless seduction game in which their masculinity (look ma, no hands, I can do it) is demonstrated again and again. Some men loose in our society are versions of the flasher who repeatedly takes out his penis in public to assure himself it is still there. Common sense would tell us that the numbers of such men have not actually grown but that the army and the priesthood no longer absorb so many of them. Emotional fuckwittage, a condition we can't actually count, is more to be pitied than censored. Such boy men are sad sacks and ought to be forced to wear dog tags that identify them as such so that women don't waste their precious time with them.

But they have their equal in females who are avoiding men, because men tend to be bossy or because men remind them of all their bad experience with daddies or stepdaddies, etc., or because the heart has died of malnutrition and can't be revived under any circumstances. It's not just men who are unsure of their masculinity, there are women who are unsure of their femininity and aren't the least bit sure they really want a man to play with their heads and test the limits of their emotional strength. In other eras there were always nuns and spinsters and maiden aunts and now we have relabeled them as career women, professional women, independent souls who can barely water a plant much less mash bananas for a child. These are the modern old maids who say they want to marry but don't really mean it, or who say they don't want to marry and really do mean it. It is politically incorrect to point out such women but they have their own form of emotional fuck-wittage and make their own contribution to the communal unhappiness.

Some men over thirty who are unattached may be emotional idiots but it seems more likely that many of them are also lonely, tired of waking up next to a stranger, tired of relationships that seem promising but that end abruptly with unexplained cold shoulders. It is most probable that they too are tired of presenting themselves to a new person, telling the same stories of how they were lost on a class trip or what their mothers did or did not do to or for them. It is almost certain that men too worry about being left out of the coupling, single forever and somehow stigmatized. "Well is he gay or isn't he? Is he just emotionally unable?" Men too fear dying alone with no one to hold their hand when a bad diagnosis is pronounced. While there are men who are not suited for marriage, for whom the idea of fidelity is a hurdle to be jumped over or run around, it seems reasonable that most of our sons and most of our brothers are afflicted by the same needs and fears, wishes and hopes that drive women to accept the next date and the one after that.

The problem of commitment, the thirty-something man or woman who hesitates again and again and refuses to bind himself or herself to another, that we see in the modern world stems in part from the bad marriages so many have seen in their parents' generation. The child of divorce has no happily-ever-after delusion to hang on to. But if the child of divorced parents is so afraid of repeating his parents' mistake, so without confidence in his or her own ability to do it better, then they are divorce victims second generation, emotionally impoverished, cramped. It is understandable that the child of divorce should fear marriage but the alternative is a restless search for a relationship considered puncture proof, perfect, and with guarantees built in. Since there are no guarantees, since no relationship can promise to last or promise to be good to the last drop, the searcher is ever after a person pressing against the window, staring at those inside, afraid to open the door. The men who won't commit, who seem to haunt our urban bars like bats hanging in the rafters, flying down from time to time to hear the women scream, are really a pitiful lot so afraid of losing they won't play the game.

If parents have failed in their marriages, if remarriages have made their offspring suffer, if the life of the older generation has been mangled by bitterness, anger and economic troubles children will quite reasonably be hesitant to jump into the same waters in which the sharks took the limbs off their mothers and fathers. Yet if they stay out of the water they won't experience another person as a partner, there for them, next to them, companion for life.

You've Come a Long Circle, Baby

When I was of dating age a boy came to the door and brought me a flower to wear on the shoulder of my dress and took me to a movie and brought me home at the appointed hour. I could kiss him or not as I inclined. I wouldn't allow his hands to stray. I would bite his tongue if it went too far. I didn't want to be one of those girls who were talked about in locker rooms. I knew the stakes were high and someone I might love might reject me all because of what I had allowed on a Saturday night years before and didn't really mean. But my own young teenage girls went out on Friday and Saturday nights in packs like a band of roving minstrels, off to parties without dates but with goings-on. I knew there were goings-on. No boy appeared at the door and showed his face until on occasion I would find one sleeping on the couch or overhear one calling his mother on the phone in the middle of the night.

My daughters began their sexual lives with gawky boys in braces. They loved with a terrible seriousness that seemed all absorbing, sometimes good, sometimes not. They took risks with their bodies. They rode the subways late at night. If we imposed some surface order that order was undone behind our backs around the corner in someone else's house. Sex and love came early. Friendships were intense and burned with meaningful whispers in telephones in other rooms. I would not say they were sweet and pure girls. I would not say they were unusual for their kind. They knew far more than I did at their age. They knew about birth control and they knew about sexually transmitted diseases and they knew about loyalty and betrayal. But for what purpose, to what avail?

In college great loves ended and new ones began. They lived in dorm rooms with this one or that: underwear spread over the pillows, men in the bathrooms and signs of last night's party, beer bottles, cigarette butts, pretzels scattered across the floor. Sometimes they were sad and sometimes they were not.

My daughters had a girlhood in which anticipation was quickly followed by experience. The teddy bears are still sitting on the bed when a boy jumps under the covers. The capacity to love and remain loyal is tested along with one's skill in geometry, and one's birth control pills or condoms are carried in the same backpack with the gym socks. Perhaps this makes this generation wiser and more sophisticated as they enter the marriage field, enter adult relationships. But perhaps it makes them fearful, cautious, or indifferent or casual or closed off or too open to new experience. It was a terrible world when young women thought they had to be married at twenty-two without any sexual experience or all was over for them. But is it better now or have we just substituted the tyranny of one set of social customs for the tyranny of another?

Virginity was a burden easily put down. There were no consequences for its loss. This is progress of sorts. On the other hand I did not notice great joy in my children's teenage years or ease with their bodies or confidence in their fates. If they had turned into a form of Samoan native that danced through the mating rituals with flowers in their hair I would have been

pleased. As it was one worry was replaced by others, less iden-
tifiable, more pervasive, and still toxic for human happiness.

So I think of my mother who so devoutly believed in virginity and so worried about mine and I wonder if it was easier
that way. If women today were married early, before their
twenty-second birthday, and knew only their husbands and did
not have the long time that my daughters have to experiment,
to find out who they really are, what they really like, would
they have been spared the odd broken heart, the terrible tear
of relationships ending, the wounds of pride and tests of character that my daughters have experienced? Would it have been
simpler to have been wed without so much information about
oneself and the other sex? Or was it worse that way? Or is it
hard no matter which way we arrange our courtship patterns?

We cannot put teenage sexuality back in the bottle once
having let it out. In parts of this country they are preaching
abstinence as a form of birth control and they are holding ceremonies for born-again virgins. Except for isolated tiny pock-
ets of religious conservatives this idea is as popular as
replacing the family car with the horse and buggy. Where conservatives rule sex information is watered down and teenagers
graduate from high school pregnant and shame prevails and
marriages are no happier than anywhere else in the world.
Teenage hormones being what they are, teenage exposure to
sexually suggestive material in movies and on the web being
what it is, there isn't a chance in hell that daydreaming will
suffice. With sexual activity comes love and with love comes
disaster and so it is.

The social conservatives do have a point. After all how many boyfriends can Ally McBeal win and lose without going entirely crazy? Obviously she has already exceeded that number. Candace Bushnell in "Sex in the City" gives us a sharp and nasty view of women in their thirties obsessed with dress and money and finding the right man and dreading the doldrums of marriage with kids whom they do not love or wish to care for. Her book is chock full of brand names and prices for goods. We see a group of women whose misery is well dressed and whose style is not in question. But we also see a kind of grim unhappy female something like J. D. Salinger's mismarried drunken lady that he describes in his short story "Uncle Wiggily in Connecticut" or like Dorothy Parker's "Big Blonde," a woman who missed out on love and marriage. If I believed that life had to be like that, like a Candace Bushnell column, like a Dorothy Parker story, as filled with anomie as Ann Beattie, as bitter and cruel as any sexual relationship in any Philip Roth novel, I would flee to the northernmost villages of Alaska and open a last stop trading post for hunters about to step out on the ice floe.

Most of us have not given up on the idea of romantic love and happy marriage despite the odds against it. But what we have done is postponed the moment of choice for another decade into our lives. This postponement gives us time to grow up, to mature, to test out our real desires and to make our first mistakes and learn from them. So much to the good. But at the same time this long courtship process, which can involve a change of partners again and again, threatens female fertility, is wearying, bruising and tough to live through. This is a social change that might better be abandoned or at least rethought.

After college in graduate schools my daughters each began to live with a particular man and set up house with dishes and shared furniture and lamps. These relationships were like first marriages, sort of, they required the same work and patience and flexibility that my generation's first marriages demanded. These relationships too left broken hearts, sorrow like no other, fear of the future as always, guilt of course, when they broke up. Even years later the scar on their lives was visible.

There is no evidence that the long periods of living with the wrong man that so many young women experience in their twenties grants them better odds when they do get married. The living-with arrangement is certainly good for paying the high rents in our urban centers but it may prove to be a bad way to go for young people. The breakups are anguishing and hardly less difficult and scarring than divorce itself. Books and furniture have to be divided. Friends are split between the couple. New living situations have to be found. The sense of failure or disappointment in the self or the partner is pro-found. Young men and women don't recover or rebound from these breakups with instant buoyancy. Depressions, visits to psychiatrists, doses of Prozac follow on the heels of these breakups. True there will be no fight over money and property. There will be no lasting aftershocks of these relationships since they most often do not involve children. But what we do have after the common breakup is a host of young adults more afraid for their future, less confident than they were before they moved in with their lover. They take a while to recover, to reconnect to new partners. None of this is joyous. None of this seems to be an improvement on the social situation that existed before men and women could shack up together in full view of their parents without fear of criticism. Edith Wharton's naive state when she married contributed to the disaster that followed. But not being naive has its own drawbacks and since marital disasters have not disappeared we need to look further for causes.

It wouldn't be a bad idea if it became uncool to live together before marriage. Sometimes it works out just right but sometimes it doesn't. Marriage may be something one can't rehearse. Marriage may be something that unlike a novel does not need a first draft. It may be a leap of faith whenever you do it, even after years of splitting the rent. If sharing a bathroom on a regular basis became a social taboo would the couple really enter marriage at a disadvantage? Would marriage then be like getting into a barrel with your intended and jumping into waters running over Niagara Falls? Or is it that way now even after years of common-law domesticity? There is no evidence yet that marriages that happen after the couple has lived together are in fact stronger than those entered into with more speed. Without doubt an insistence on separate residences while single might spare us some major disruption pain and return the age at which people get married to a more reasonable one, given our biology and our urgent needs to connect to another.

This is not said out of some sexual puritanism, some desire to make marriage the only place where a man or a woman can find erotic happiness. All the attitudes of the earlier era towards premarital sex were based on a presumption of sin in sexual activity. Where's the sin when consenting adults equipped with proper birth control ignore the flickering TV and enjoy the evening's possibilities? I don't much like repression, hormones backing up into the brain and screwing up the plumbing. But yes, this groping around in the dark can be overdone. There is certainly such a thing as too much careening about, too much sharing of one's body. One piece of chocolate cake is delicious. The entire cake can give you the bellyache of a lifetime. Sure, sex can debase the spirit if it is casual, impersonal, and leads to increased aloneness: the feeling that follows automatically on false or illusionary connection. Of course if you're a novelist like Philip Roth all that carnal thrashing about can lead to royalties and literary prizes and such but for the rest of us, we may be simply thrashing ourselves.

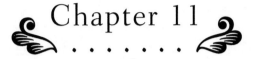

Chapter 11

Hints, Not Instructions

So you don't need to get married to have children and you certainly don't need to get married to have sex and you don't need to get married to make a mark in this world. Why on earth would anybody bother? And why would marriage still be on the agenda of career women and men of a certain age, filling our television screens, providing endings for our comedies? Maybe it's the fact that no one has figured out a better way to raise children. Think of it—two parents, one roof, a family. That idea still stirs us, inspires wistful sighs, and cynical as we may be, it touches something deep and maybe corny within. We all have a somewhat embarrassing Hallmark-card image of home printed indelibly in our brains. There it is, the way we wanted our own homes to be, the life we want to lead, connected to others, protected and protecting. The ideal itself of marriage and family survives like a treasure hidden in the hold of a ship down there at the bottom of the cultural sea. It survives despite well-deserved feminist attacks and the perks of the sexual revolution and in vitro fertilization as well as the real pictures we have of our own so often less-than-happy childhood homes.

The fact is that no one has come up with a better idea for raising the next generation. No one has created an adequate substitute for the love of a man for his wife and a wife for her man and the fierce connection of both of them to their children. The Christian "family values" spokespersons may say that this is what God wants or commanded. They may speak of traditional sex roles as if they were holy sacraments, but most of us yearn for real families without God telling us we should or what the division of labor within them should be. Most of us wish our own families were better, stronger, wiser than they were. But we have no intention of roaming the earth ever free, ever wild. We come from a domestic species. We want a hearth. What makes me shiver with fear for my daughters is that they may never have one.

People marry without a manual, at least without one that is fail-safe. They do it knowing the odds are not good. They do it, at least some do it, with the full intention of joining the ranks of the happily married. Misfortune, adultery, missed connections, growing apart will happen to someone else, of that they are sure. We marry somewhat the way we face our own deaths. Reality lurks, haunts, casts shadows, but in no way prevents us from enjoying a splash in the pool, a kiss behind a potted palm, a boat ride in twilight. We manage to convince ourselves that we are immune to mortal tragedy, at least for a time. This is one of our great human gifts.

The traditional family values people assume that if marriage were the only place for sex and if women, virgins when they marry, would only stay home and do their husbands' bidding as commanded in the Bible and if people put their family ahead of the distractions of liquor, gambling, drugs, and sexual diversions all would be well. If abortion were illegal and sex-hygiene classes preached chastity then all would be well. The spokespersons for the Bible Belt want to erase the sexual revolution and the feminist movement from our culture.

The Amish want us to go back to the farm. The ultraorthodox Jews want us to wear the clothes that were de rigueur in the thirteenth century in Poland. But time stands still only in the grave and the many injustices that plagued the traditional family spoke of bad values rather than good ones. The double standard that allowed men more freedom than women is a yoke around the neck most women will no longer voluntarily wear. The forced marriages that led to unhappy lives that the lack of abortion provoked, the unwanted children born to women who could not or would not care for them, the deaths from botched abortions when it was illegal to help a woman end a pregnancy even if she had been raped, those family values will not do anymore, they did not make people happier, stronger, wiser. They oppressed in the name of social order. They were tyrannical in the name of conformity. The assumption that men could have mistresses from a lower class that prevailed in many parts of this country, that women should be bored and allow their talents for business, medicine, law, the arts to lie fallow so their husbands could dominate them is one that most modern women will never accept. Most families can no longer really afford the traditional division of labor even if they want to.

But that doesn't mean that we are not groping our way to a new family with a strong system of values and beliefs that will support it through the years. The new man who can change a diaper and the new woman who can go to school and become whatever her abilities allow her to become can still form bonds of unbreakable strength and commit to each other in a way that is splashed with sanctity, and soaked in hope.

If one of my daughters were to tell me she was planning to marry a suitable suitor, someone she knew over the course of enough years to recognize the pitfalls and the irritations that lay ahead, blood would rush to my head. My cup would run over, pleasure spilling down its sides. I would feel tearful with delight. I would without reason or caution, without clarity of mind or an ounce of healthy skepticism, dive right into that oasis of peace, that island of hope that is refuge from reality where the mother and the bride plan the wedding.

No red-blooded American child wants advice from the parental generation. But I would give it anyway. The worse that could happen is it would fall on deaf ears. What I know comes from experience good and bad and what I know ought to be taken along on the honeymoon and given a place of honor on the mantle and remembered through the years. What will actually happen to my sage words is quite another matter.

I know our capacity for selfishness is enormous and our basic anxiety, "I am not loved, I am alone in the world, something terrible will happen to me," rises again and again long after childhoods end right through marriage and makes it hard for us to trust another and makes it hard for us to even begin to consider the needs of another person. Old angers, fears, misunderstandings jump into the marriage bed. We have no effective fumigant or anti-toxic spray. So all rational schemes for succeeding in marriage are undermined by the nutty souls we bring with us wherever we go. Nevertheless I'm writing this letter now because my words (my pearls aside) are the family jewels and I want them in a safe place.

Letter to Any Daughter Who Will One Day Decide to Get Married, Maybe

I know you don't want to hear from me on this subject but this is my book and you can't stop me. This is my advice to you. Don't read any further if you don't want to.

The basic step of the marriage dance is to find a way to stay close to another while retaining one's own individual self. That means that you can't merge into the other so completely that there is no you left. At the same time you can't go on just doing as you please, just following your star, just flashing your pretty wings about the universe.

Think of the clinging of couples that have merged into one being. It sets the teeth on edge. Think of those couples who finish each other's sentences, who have grown to look alike, who have the same opinions and do everything together. They are like pigeons on a ledge, cooing and fluff-

ing their feathers. But sooner or later one of them may rebel
and fly off in search of another pigeon, sooner or later one
of them may want to visit the North Pole or both of them
may spend their entire lives with whole parts of their minds
and hearts withered from disuse. When two become one
some of the strengths of each are lost. They become less
interesting to their mate because who can tell one pigeon
from another? In fact this two-into-one business makes
them dreary. They lose whatever shine they may once have
had. Why shouldn't their different temperaments and passions be of interest to each other rather than a threat to the
unity of the marriage? When your mirror is your mate something can crack.

Don't get married when you are feeling weak and
unsure of your worth. Don't get married to someone who feels
weak and unsure of his or her worth. Don't get married
to someone who is competing with you. Don't get married to
someone who has never loved anyone else. (This rules out
teenage marriages.) Don't get married to someone without
the capacity for hard work. Be wary of someone obsessed
with their weight or someone who must have muscles the
size of pie plates. Don't get married to someone whose world
view is in conflict with yours. Don't ever ever marry planning on changing your mate. If he is a religious fanatic now
he will be one later. If he has values you find repulsive don't
think he'll see the light because of your shine. If he is a
nervous wreck, a heavy drinker, a man with a paranoid attitude towards his boss, the policeman at the corner, our government representatives, don't think he'll gentle down if he

sleeps in your bed. More likely you will be up all night. Don't imagine that marriage itself is a form of sex therapy. It isn't. If he tells you he's had a long history of gay experiences but everything will be different with you, be flattered if you must but don't be tempted to marry him. You're wonderful but not that wonderful.

Have I set the barrier too high? Have I eliminated all prospects? This is only a rough guide. You have your own don'ts, people who are off limits for a variety of other reasons. This one seems too soft, this one seems too weird, this one seems stupid and that one cold. I know you don't need my antennae out there sending out signals on your behalf.

The man I want for you is both sweet and strong. I want him to weather the bad times. I want him to be ambitious and to care about others in this world. I want him to be capable of earning a living. I want that of you too. I want him to like children and look forward to having his own. I want him to like some of the movies you like and some of the music you like and it would be a bonus if he was able to plug things in and make the VCR work. I would like him to protect you from wild beasts and comfort you when one has sunk his teeth into you in the dark of the forest where you were traveling without him. I would like him to be smart. But smart is not the equivalent of good and smart alone does not tell you that a man has the energy or the will or the grace to survive in the world. Some smart men are depressed and crazy and useless. So are some smart women. Some smart men don't care about what they are doing. If lawyers they don't like the law, if doctors they are bored with their practices, if professors they are no longer interested in their students, if businessmen they no longer get high from the deal. If poets they have stopped writing. Avoid them all. There is something seriously amiss in their souls.

Of course I would happily accept anyone you choose. But I have to admit I would like you to marry someone who comes from a family not totally strange to us. I know that is not a very American idea. I know that the melting pot is on the stove and there's not much I or any other parent can do about it. But it would be easier to know that the things you care about your spouse has also been taught. Wouldn't it be a good thing if his father had voted for the very same presidential candidates that yours had? Wouldn't it be good if your religion and his religion were the same so that the family you create could fold into the particular identity within the American weave that you already have? There are so many sharp and difficult differences between people who are next-door neighbors, attend the same house of worship, went to the same schools that it seems to me unnecessary to add tensions from opposing holidays, opposing loyalties, opposing memories.

Feel free to ignore this statement. There is no real rational convincing reason that my attachments to my group must be yours. But should it turn out that way I wouldn't be sorry. Not at all.

I am expecting you not to marry like a screaming teenybopper at a concert. I want you to know what you need to do in a clear practical way to give your marriage an odds on chance of success.

*There is compromise—be prepared to compromise espe-
cially on things that really matter. This year on vacation
we'll go to the beach because I know you love the ocean and
next year we'll go to the mountains because I have childhood memories of forests and pine needles and dark lakes.
Please don't be pig-headed or selfish or think what you want
you must have. Learn to give a little on your own absolutes.
Accept his friend, the one who bores you. Accept his love of
bowling, you might grow to like it. But make sure that the
compromising isn't all on your part. Be graceful when he
bends towards your point of view.*

*On the other hand there is independence. Take a course
in Greek literature because you always wanted to read* The
Odyssey *in the language in which it was written. He'll
accept that you'll be out every Tuesday night. Don't be
mean about his old friend who wants him to visit without
you. Independence can't be just yours to enjoy. It's his too.
Figure it out. Work it out. Grow up.*

The word intimacy *is vastly overused. You need it, yes,
but what exactly is it? Those who have it don't use the word
and those who are searching for it may never find it. It con-
sists perhaps of the daily work of connection. Let him tell
you more about his aunt, the one he hardly ever talks about.
What actually happened that summer he stayed with her?
When he is worried about work, listen. When you are worried about work, talk to him. When he feels sick bring him
his favorite flavor ice cream. When you are sick feel free to
ask him to come home early. All of this is obvious and
requires no special knowledge. The electricity that binds*

one to another is made up of energy, yours and his, directed towards each other in kindness, affection and concern. This is not a trick. You don't need a book to tell you about it. You need to be as unafraid of him as he needs to be unafraid of you. You need to admire him, even when he is not entirely admirable. He must do the same for you. Connection is sex but not just sex. Connection is allowing closeness, putting aside pride and vulnerability and fear of exposure and putting out your hand and taking his and lying on the sofa and watching an old movie. It's sharing gossip and analyzing the behavior of people you know. It's talking about your parents the way you would hardly ever with a friend and never with your parents. It's lying silently near each other and not talking sometimes.

And through all this there is discipline. Here is a real sticking point. You can't do everything you want all the time because you have to think of him and what he wants and when you have children it gets worse. Then you have to put yourself third or fourth or fifth. You have to get up in the middle of the night when called. You have to spend hours of your day focused on others. No one finds this easy. Be prepared to feel restless under this yoke. You would like to move to the country but it would be too long a commute for him. He would like to go dancing till four in the morning but you have to get up at seven. I know you know how to work hard. You've been tested. You don't party all night at least not all of the time. You have always had discipline. This takes discipline too, more than anything you've ever done before.

I'm thinking about china. My mother's china and the china you might want for a wedding present. I'm thinking of porcelain piled up in the cabinets waiting for holidays, for parties, for celebrations. Your china murmuring for months on end unnoticed in your cabinets will not betray your materialism or any other evil. It will have other purposes. It isn't the actual pattern of china that will matter or the style you pick. Some of your china will have passed from my grandmother, to my mother, to you. Some of it will come with your wedding. One day these dishes too will belong to a future you can't imagine. Owning china isn't merely a sign that you no longer live out of a backpack or move about like a drifting leaf. Its significance lies in the fact that the china on the table will hold the history of your family, the hands that fixed the food that was placed on the china, the hands that washed the china, the hands that replaced the china in the cabinet for the next occasion, the hands that picked up the forks and knives and put them down. This china will shine with the tales that were told around the table, the unease of the family that increased or abated around that table. The china cabinet is a kind of diary. You receive china as a gift when you marry not because you don't have any plates to eat off of now but because the tale of the china, the linking of the generations, comforts us all, the dead, the living, the ones who come later.

Don't despair. I'm almost done. What I want for you is a man who will feel that you are his best friend and he is yours. I want for you a man who will do his share economically and in the home. I want for you a man who will be tender to his children and hold their interests above all else. I want a man who will say interesting things to you as the years go by, whose mind will not turn to wood, who will not lose his energy and interest in the world outside. Who will go with you to theater and museums and parks, perhaps parks in foreign countries. I want a man who will not betray you and one you will not be tempted to betray. I want for you a partner who will not despair until there is real reason to despair. I want you to have a man whose bad habits make you smile.

I want you to have a man who will not be felled by accident or disease. (You have no control over this—I have no control over this. I'm wishing anyway. I'm begging fate.) I want you to wake in the morning glad to see him and fall asleep at night with his breathing beside you. I also have an additional want based on sad old tales. I want you to be with a man who will perceive danger if it comes and will plan ahead with you. If you need to escape in time I want you to be with a man who will not panic but will not deny danger. I also want that from you. I am not asking too much, just what any mother would want for her daughter.

If only I could bend my spirit over yours, chase away all threats, internal, external to your kingdom, I would, you know I would. But the truth is that you are on your own. Soon you will reach the horizon's edge and I won't be able to see you anymore which was always the plan from the very beginning.

Your mother

P.S. The china that you will receive from your grand-mother is missing much of its gold leaf. That's because I have exercised a Darwinian approach to plates. Only those that can survive the dishwasher, survive.

Haven't You Anything Good to Say About Marriage?

There are however ways in which marriage can serve to heal old wounds or at least see to it that they become less intrusive on the present. When I first met my spouse his back would go out every eight months or so. He sat many hours in a chair listening to patients. He was stiff all the time. He would lie on his office floor in pain and hobble about for days. After we had been married for a few years, his back, the same anatomical spine as before, same hours spent sitting and listening, served him day in and day out without spasm, without pain, without bother. I claimed that I had magically cured his back problem. This was not accomplished through voodoo or because I have a healer's touch or because I gave him a copper bracelet. This shift in his body tension occurred as our home became a safe place, a shelter for both of us, and in this process affection gradually replaced the anger that can cramp the muscles or pinch the vessels of the head or back until a severe ache occurs.

The gradual healing of the partner's old wounds from childhood, the tempering of them into minor symptoms, the easing of wracking existential anxiety, this is the long-term work of the marriage and if each partner steadies the other then the marriage itself gains resilience and strength. If a husband is kinder than a father, if a woman loves a man's body while his own mother ignored him or his older brother taunted him then there is a chance that the old angers, the old tightness, the old suspiciousness will melt slowly away. Marriage is itself a place to ease guilt, to temper rage, to gain the courage to explore new directions.

One of my daughters was afraid to drive a car. She is a cautious type who is always on the alert for falling objects or potential crashes. After a number of years in a serious relationship with a man who likes going places in his vehicle she decided she wanted to drive herself around and began to take lessons. When she finally got her driver's license, some ten years after most Americans achieve that milestone, we all knew that something had shifted in her soul and her world had become a less fearful place. If this couple ever decided to get married she could without doubt pilot a Boeing 747.

But what of new wounds? There always are some. A job is lost. A promotion expected falls through. A child disappoints at school. Illness threatens. Parents sicken and die. Finances go badly. Insults to the mind and body are hard to avoid. Deep troubles like the illness of a child or one of the partners chill to the bone. What keeps a marriage going in hard times?

The easy answer is love. If you just love your partner sufficiently then the rough seas toss you together instead of pulling you apart. The easy answer is far too easy. In fact it's silly. It takes a lot more than mere love to support and maintain marriage through foul periods. It requires grit. It takes patience and discipline and a little bit of luck, also fear of change helps, prompting people just to hang in there. Habits are hard to break and one's spouse and one's life with one's spouse is definitely a habit-ridden matter. This unromantic fact alone may keep you from fleeing your home when things are going badly.

Love is a word for the host of emotions we attach to our partners and some of them aren't exactly loving. We need to admire our spouse but after a while no spouse is bathed in idealistic light. We know that the clay feet are waiting right there in the closet with the shoes. We know that the flaws we suspected before marriage are in fact real and possibly worse than we had imagined and we are attached anyway, care anyway, need the other anyway. Romantic love takes on other patinas, it becomes shellacked with friendship, encrusted with small practical matters: "where are the garden shears, what did you do with last year's tax papers, you're going to lose your teeth if you don't floss, you were the one who wanted the children to have a dog," etc. Romantic love changes under the weight of shared memories and shared obligations. It doesn't sit still like a vase on a shelf but it moves through our days like the light that fills the room, differently at different hours of the day.

Sex between partners is a fine cement for a relationship. If sex is good it lends a glow to all other matters. It makes it possible to absorb and tolerate disappointments about the spouse in other areas. All right she can't keep the checkbook, all right she stays too late at her office, all right he has a terrible temper, he has no patience with his son and we disagree on how to punish the child or on how to educate the child but we are good together in bed, which trumps most other matters usually at least for a while. But in times of real trouble sex, like food, is not much on anyone's mind. If a child is ill or money is scarce or depression or cancer has entered the home sex is not the cure or the issue. Patience helps. Courage helps. Character matters. Attitude matters. This will get better. We will figure a way out of this. We are miserable now but we will make it through together. Those thoughts turn the couple towards each other instead of away.

Couples can take turns despairing and falling apart. But if both of them collapse at the same time the marriage itself may fall. In bad times both partners need a comforter, a reassurer, a calm voice that predicts light at the end of the tunnel or at the least speaks the words that need to be said. That part needs to be played by someone, not necessarily the same someone all the time. Some people are like turtles who when they feel danger near pull in their heads and hope the hardness of their shells will suffice to save them. This leaves the other partner who is already upset more upset, lonelier than before and without support. Some people deny until they can't that disaster is on the doorstep. They don't want to talk about it, not at all. This may be good survival technique if lost alone in the woods but it is not a good way to protect a marriage.

The style of each couple is different but one of the partners has to keep the lines open, if not always at least sometimes so that the one who is overwhelmed can speak of his or her fear or pain and the other one can be if not a comfort at least a presence, a hand, a leg pressing against a leg. I saw such a couple in my doctor's office. They were grey-haired. He had a cane. She was reading a magazine. He kept wiping his face with a handkerchief. She kept locking and unlocking her ankles and shifting in her seat. The wait was long. He reached out his hand and patted her shoulder. She seemed not to notice. But she moved her chair a little closer to his. She opened her bag and took out a candy and offered it to him. He shook his head. She pressed her foot onto his foot gently and let it rest there. Her shoulder was against his. The nurse called her name and they both went into the office.

Loss

My mate is older than I am and while he is in perfect health I know the facts about life span and such and I may lose him before he loses me. I think of life without him. I think of lying in our bed without his arm over my body, without his breathing next to me and I think I could not do it. I would not do it. I think of having dinner alone at our table and I think I could not do it. I would not do it. I think of being in our apartment and looking at the wallpaper he doesn't want changed and I think of looking at his books and his clothes and his not being there and I know I could not do it. I think of him watering our jade plant or talking to his patients on the phone, his voice low so I can't make out the words. I think of him by my side at the beach reading. I think of his returning from the antique store he haunts carrying yet another model ship, its sails unfurled, its miniature mounted guns already counted, for our already extremely nautical home. What if it was over: our life together? As I imagine this I feel a return of the devastation I felt as a child when my parents were fighting in the other room, as if the spaces in-between the furniture had grown suddenly vast, shadows everywhere, as if the windows reflected no light, as if I am being deprived of oxygen. I recognize that feeling.

I suppose the price you have to pay for a marriage that hasn't been half bad is very high at the end. Maybe I wouldn't recover. He doesn't like to hear me say this. He wants me to enjoy every year of life I can. He insists that I'll be fine. We'll see. I may yet die first. This is the only good reason I can find not to get married: If you aren't married you can't lose your mate.

So Really—Why Should Anyone Get Married?

Marriage is not the only way to be respectable these days and social power is possessed by those who mock the rules (rock and rap stars, movie stars, wealthy men) and social disapproval carries no real sting in urban America and less than it used to across the land. We cannot say that marriage, conventional marriage, is necessary for the stability of the society or the success of the individual child. Marriage needs another defense if it is to remain a part of our lives.

And it has one. Marriage can answer one human problem better than any other solution yet divined. It can assuage our loneliness. It can give us a companion through the years. It can ease our self-centeredness and wear away at our faults by combining us with another who has other needs, other strengths. The twoness of marriage is the only remaining reason to hold on to this institution and expect it to enrich our lives. The twoness, the closeness is a breeding ground for trouble but it is also the reason that marriage remains with us and will remain with us until our very human nature is altered by some evolutionary process that turns us back into birds or fish.

Yes, you could have serial partners, a sense of closeness begun, lost, renewed, lost and a new partner taken to heart. If you did this you might have many different kinds of experience, you might learn about a variety of matters, tango with this one and math with another, you might live in this part of the country or that, you might have a dog in one relationship and a sailboat in another. This preserves your freedom. It keeps options open. When you marry for life you close so many doors behind you, rooms that contain not only other bodies but other ways of life, you will never travel across country in a van or you will never have a meal in the best restaurant in Paris. If you value your freedom to move above consistency, connection, knowing, really knowing another, then you will have many relationships and none that are permanent, or even intended to be. In *The Dying Animal* Philip Roth's sex-obsessed David Kepesh makes an argument for freedom, for the deliciousness of the taste of different women, for the anti-bourgeois lifestyle of experimentation and variety. He sees all marriage as the slow lifelong acquittal of a debt, as did Edith Wharton. He with the benefit of the sexual revolution would agree that marriage was a crime against human nature. But

Kepesh is not a happy man. He is jealous and obsessed with the body of a woman many years younger than he. He has created his own psychological prison in which he is focused on this one woman and her beauty and feels constantly deprived and unjustly treated. The irony here is that freedom is not so easy to obtain. Our own inclination towards suffering can make life a living hell without help of state or clergy. Kepesh argues well for the glories of the sexual revolution and he mocks his son who is trying to be faithful to the wife he met in college and married when she got pregnant. But the truth is that Kepesh is a nervous wreck, obsessing about a woman or her breasts in a way that produces agony not joy, facing old age alone, using sex when he can as a shield to protect him from his barren soul and the death he sees coming. (What a nice irony—she dies instead of him—if this is the aging author's sacrifice to appease the gods—it won't work.)

The familiar is never as exciting as the new. Falling in love many times over may be a pleasure, a new sensation, offer a life ever tingling with erotic possibility. But this has got to be hard on the spirit. It involves emotional pain, separation, loneliness, new beginnings and new beginnings again. It is forced on some of us, this beginning again, on the divorced and the widower or the widow for example, but as a design for living, an intended design, its flaws are obvious. I was never so alone as between my marriages. I was never so aware that I had no extra pair of hands in the house, no extra paycheck to count on, no one to care if I was blue, green or red. I know that strong women and strong men are not supposed to need all those things. They say that a mentally healthy person can stand alone, possess this much-vaunted quality of autonomy. I think autonomy, if it means not sharing someone else's bed over many many years, is a hard sell. I don't want any part of it. I don't want it for my daughters. I suspect there are no autonomous women or men only those who have adjusted to the absence of the other, an absence many of them assume is only temporary. Nuns and priests are compensated for their loss by the strong community of their fellows, by the unique purpose of their vocation and the special place it gives them among mortals. The rest of us who have lost our mates or never found them may whistle a brave tune, but the musical notes are simply noise to keep the evil spirits in their place.

In other eras when the divorce rate was negligible many families were headed by one parent too. This is because the death rate was so high. Today sociologist Arlene Skolnick reports that three-quarters of all people die after their sixty-fifth birthday: "In 1850 only 2% of the population lived past sixty-five. This current longevity changes everything. It means that a baby girl today has a better chance of reaching sixty than her counterpart born in 1870 would have had of reaching her first birthday. For the first time in history the average couple has more parents living than it has children." Now we parent our adult children, which is a mixed blessing and something of a surprise. In 1900 one out of four children under the age of fifteen lost a parent. One out of sixty-two lost both. Now only one out of 1,800 children are orphans. Many people who study population statistics have pointed out that the statistical curve of rising divorce rates matches the curve of the lowered death rate. In other words the less death, the more divorce. Our family values are no worse than ever. We just live long enough to wear them out. In that sense the high divorce rate does not produce an entirely new way of raising children. It carries within it the good news of our longer lives and raised expectations for greater happiness. The society did not crumble because so many children were raised by single parents or in institutions. This was considered normal. The longer time that married couples can be expected to live with each other puts new pressures on marriage. Both mates experience their lives changing and their personal needs shifting many times over.

To be sick and alone is terrible. To be promoted at work, to receive a prize or simple praise and have no one to share the good news with diminishes the happiness that belongs to the occasion. To be afraid and not have anyone to reassure you is like falling down a well, no rescuers hovering above. To have the day begin and end without a pressure against your skin, without a word from someone who knows what matters to you, without a caress from someone who knows what place on your spine needs rubbing, this is hard. Yes, you can say loneliness is better than being with the wrong person and that is true, except the reason not to be married to the wrong person is clearer when you see that the wrong person is keeping you from the right person. You can say that we all are too dependent on another and should learn to hold our own in the world without a companion. But it is better if there is someone you can wake when a nightmare leaves you confused and tumbled in your sheets. It is better if there is someone whose deeds in the world please you, worry you, excite you as much as your own. The twoness of things which is what a good love comes down to is the life enhancer of old people, the erotic stimulant of young, the prod to reproduce, the means to reproduce, the motive for the long effort of child rearing, the pleasure of accomplishment.

That's why people who have been divorced remarry. That's why they go to bars looking for a friendly soul in a desirable body rather than an evening's diversion at the movies. That's what the personal ads are promising. I will stop your loneliness if you will stop mine. Marriage holds out equal promise to both partners. If you are someone I cannot hurt without hurting myself, then you are safe in my bed. If I am someone you need then you will never leave me. If often the promise falls short then a person can try again.

Marital anxiety, do we need it, should we do it, may have infected many of us. The only cure is bravery, daring, leaping the way one took one's first head-first dive into the deep end of the pool. The loneliness of modern men and women is fierce. None of our social organizations are tight enough, if ever they were, to cradle us and support us through our days. Our belief systems are rattled and ragged. God is rarely at our side and if He is He keeps his own counsel. We need at least a hand in our hand. That is the justification for marriage.

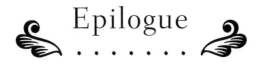

Epilogue

One of my daughters has gone to a wedding of a college friend in Naples with the man she has been romantically entangled with for a number of years. How many years? I try to count them but I can't remember exactly. Is it three or four? They are planning to visit Naples and the ruins of Pompeii. What if they live together and never marry? Am I so old-fashioned, so traditional a person that I would wish it otherwise? What if they have a disastrous fight while traveling and decide to leave each other? I think how sad my daughter would be. How she would lose weight and be unable to sleep and how many months would pass before she returned to her usual vital self, and how sad I would feel for her. "It's the times," says my spouse, "they've changed and she's independent and strong and doesn't need to be married." "You really believe that?" I ask. "Maybe," he says. He doesn't at all. He's just trying to prevent me from brooding. I am circular, repetitive, flat as a penny squashed on a railroad track, when I brood. I don't blame him for lying to me.

We are in the kitchen fixing dinner: that is, my husband is making pasta and I am opening a jar of tomato sauce. It's a warm day in the middle of May and the noises of West Side Manhattan float through the open windows of our apartment: an ambulance siren, a fire truck, a party on a nearby rooftop, Jim Lehrer on the television, his voice sincere and disinterested at the same time, the little girl who lives next door is crying in the hallway. She doesn't want Mommy and Daddy to go out for the evening. I remember when my girls did that, so long ago. What does it matter, I tell myself, if my personal DNA is not passed along? In all the vast universe mine is hardly a significant contribution. I don't care about DNA but I do feel wretched when I think of my girls not knowing what it is to have a child to raise. On the other hand since I feel wretched I think perhaps they would feel less wretched if their only worry were themselves. This conundrum, this unresolvable paradox, runs through my mind all the time. It is now background noise, like a familiar but irritating TV commercial.

The phone rings. My husband picks it up. It is our daughter from Italy. Visions of car accidents, sudden illnesses, drownings in the Mediterranean Sea fly through my head. My heart pounds. I see him turn red. I see an enormous smile on his face. My daughter's boyfriend is on the phone. Can he be a boyfriend even if he is a man in his early thirties? Our language is not up to the rapid change of our social habits. Do I see tears in my mate's eyes? They have not called to report an accident after all. They called to report an engagement.

After we hang up I realize the pasta has become pudding in its pot. My book has a happy ending in the traditional sense and I will not remind myself of what's wrong with the tradition, of how little real security lies in marriage, at least not right now. A mother is entitled to celebrate the moment, even if it means her brains have to join the pudding in the pot.